SUBMISSION ISN'T FOR SISSIES
WHY GOD CALLS US TO DO IT ANYWAY

by Kelly Wehunt

FOREWORD by Erin Davis

Cover Design by Lindsay Robinson
Formatting by Dallas E. Caldwell

Copyright © 2014 Kelly Wehunt

All rights reserved.

ISBN: 1503399176
ISBN-13: 978-1503399174

To my daughter Payton. I pray every day that you will be a woman who seeks God and submits to Him with every aspect of your life.
I love you, P.

Contents

Acknowledgements

Foreword by Erin Davis   1

Why Talk About the "S-Word"?   3

A Note to Girls: How to Use This Study   5

A Note to Mentors: How to Use This Study   7

Week One: What Exactly Is This Whole Submission Thing?

❖ Day One: May I Have The Definition Please?   12

❖ Day Two: Why should I?   21

❖ Day Three: So What Does It Look Like?   28

❖ Day Four: What Do You Want?   32

❖ Day Five: Why Submission Isn't for Sissies   36

Week Two: Submit to God

❖ Day One: Remember Who You Submit to First   45

❖ Day Two: Submitting to God with Your Anxieties   50

❖ Day Three: Submitting to God with Your Future   55

❖ Day Four: Submitting to God with Your Circumstances   60

❖ Day Five: Submitting to God with Your Appearance   67

Week Three: Submit to God by Submitting to the Authorities He has Placed in Your Life

- ❖ Day One: God Has Placed Authority Over You — 76
- ❖ Day Two: But They Don't Deserve It! — 83
- ❖ Day Three: But I Really Really Really Don't Agree! — 87
- ❖ Day Four: When It's Time to Say No — 92
- ❖ Day Five: Submitting for the Sake of the Gospel — 99

Week Four: All These Authorities... How Do I Submit to Them?

- ❖ Day One: "Children, Obey Your Parents…" — 109
- ❖ Day Two: "Slaves, Obey Your Masters…" — 115
- ❖ Day Three: "Let Every Person be Subject to the Governing Authorities…" — 124
- ❖ Day Four: "Obey Your leaders…For They Keep Watch Over Your Souls…" — 129
- ❖ Day Five: "Wives, Submit to Your Husbands…" — 138

Week Five: Submit to One Another

- ❖ Day One: Submitting to One Another With Your Thoughts — 151
- ❖ Day Two: Submitting to One Another Through Your Speech — 156
- ❖ Day Three: Submitting to One Another Through Your Actions — 162
- ❖ Day Four: Submitting to One Another in the Midst of a Fight (Part One) — 167
- ❖ Day Five: Submitting to One Another in the Midst of a Fight (Part Two) — 173

Conclusion   183

Discussion Questions   186

ACKNOWLEDGMENTS

To Chris Wehunt. You are such a godly husband and father and I am so thankful that God put you in my life. Throughout this entire process you encouraged me in so many ways. I would not have finished this book without your wisdom and guidance. I love you.

To the staff and members of Henderson Hills Baptist Church and First Baptist Church Owasso. I praise God every day that I have gotten to be a part of amazing churches. These two in particular have grown me, stretched me, and encouraged me. I am who I am today because of the time you took to teach me and shape me.

To my family and friends. I cannot think of two couples who have taught me more about what it looks like to trust and submit to God than James and Vickie Callison and Darryl and Kim Wilkerson. Also a huge thank you to my beta readers and my friends who have taught me what it looks like to submit to one another.

To Dallas and Jennifer Caldwell. Besides my husband, you were the biggest motivators for me to finish this book. On days when I wanted to quit, you encouraged me to keep going. Thank you for answering all of my millions of questions. We love you and your family so much.

FOREWORD

At twenty-one, I was a bright-eyed bride with visions of a dream marriage. Of course my version of the dream included me running the show, and my handsome husband willingly taking a backseat to my plans, my ideas, and my goals for the future.

I wish I had Kelly's book back then!

God's Word clearly teaches a concept that has become nearly taboo.

Submission.

Yes, wives are called to submit to their husbands (Ephesians 5:22-23). I can tell you from my first tumultuous years of marriage that God doesn't ask this to punish women but rather to protect them. As with all things God asks of us, wives submitting as if to the Lord and husbands loving as Christ loves the Church is marriage at its best. Doing our own thing causes lots of hurt, resentment, and chaos.

But marriage isn't the only context where God calls us to submit.

Children are asked to submit to their parents (Ephesians 6:1). We are all asked to submit to the authorities over us and recognize that God put them there (Romans 13:1). As Christians, we are called to submit to each other as a sign of our respect for Jesus (Ephesians 5:21).

But all of this is really just practice. Our human relationships are a training ground for how we will submit to the Lord. I've learned the hard way that a girl who won't submit to her human authorities will arch her back toward the commands of God. Then she will find her life to be a painful mess.

That is why the message of this book is vital for every young woman.

Yes, it's a book that will help you understand how God designed you to function in your future marriage. Yes, it will likely ease tensions at home as you learn to obey your parents with a happy heart. Yes, it will give you the tools necessary to consider others first.

But ultimately, this is a book about you and God. Why should you submit to His will for your life, especially if it goes against your own plan? Why should you obey His commands in a culture that says they are old-fashioned, out of date, and bound to spoil your fun?

Kelly has the answers. In a style that makes you feel like you're out to coffee with a great friend (caramel latte, extra whip here, please!), Kelly will drive you toward the Word of God and help you see that submission is not a four-letter word. It is part of God's plan for your good and His glory.

So grab your copy and get reading! It's gonna be a great ride!

A fan,

Erin Davis

Why Talk about the "S-word"?

"Old fashioned"

"Oppressive; puts women down"

"It means we have to do what we are told."

"I don't know much about it, but I know I don't like it."

These are just some of the answers that I received when I asked a group of high school girls what came to mind when they heard the word "submission." Every summer, twenty girls came to my home once a week to do a Bible study. During this particular study, we decided to look at passages of the Bible that spoke specifically to women. This led to several lively discussions about all kinds of topics, including modesty, inner beauty, and gossip. But nothing could have prepared me for the discussion that was about to take place. I opened up my Bible and read aloud from Ephesians 5...

"Wives, submit to your own husbands, as to the Lord..."

You could hear a pin drop in the room when the word "submit" came out of my mouth. I lowered my Bible and said, "Today, we are going to talk about submission. When I say the word submission, what comes to your mind?"

After a few moments of silence, the answers started pouring out. I was taken aback when I noticed that all of the answers had one thing in common: They were all negative. I realize that this shouldn't have surprised me. After all, this generation of girls is taught on a regular basis that a woman who allows someone else to be in control of her life is weak, and that she should constantly look for ways to make herself number one.

I was thinking about all of the lies these girls face when I heard the answer that served as the motivation for writing this book:

"Honestly, I don't know anything about it. But who cares? It doesn't apply to us anymore."

What I discovered that day is that as older women, we have performed a disservice to you, the young women that God puts around us on a daily basis. The fact that in the heart of the "Bible Belt of America," I have received responses like these repeatedly shows me that we are lacking in correct communication about the topic of submission.

It is time to stop shying away from this topic. This Bible study boldly teaches that not only does submission still apply to women today, but also it is beautiful, God-designed, and will change our lives if we choose to let it.

I pray that this Bible study becomes a tool in your hands that God uses to teach you about submission and opens the door to have conversations with others about this incredible, yet often controversial subject.

A Note to The Girls: How to Use This Study

- ❖ **Find a mentor.** I highly recommend that you find an older, Godly woman to walk through this study with you. I've designed it like this because although I wish I could write in a way that touches each of you in whatever specific environment you face… I can't. However, a spiritually more mature woman in your life can. Don't know who to ask? Talk with your Student Pastor or a staff member of your church. Or pray for God to reveal someone to you. Then, simply ask the woman if she would be interested in meeting once a week for five weeks to discuss this book. If for some reason she can't, find someone else. Don't give up! So much will be added to this study if you are able to find someone to go through it with you.

- ❖ **Soak it in.** This Bible study will take you through what submission is, who women are called to submit to (spoiler alert: It's not just about their future husbands), and how you can allow the beauty of submission to change your everyday life even now as a teenage girl. This is a five-week study in which you will go through the devotionals daily on your own then at the end of the week, you will meet with a leader to discuss the topic. Each week there are only five devotionals given, so you have two extra days a week in case you are unable to finish a devotional or fall behind schedule. Don't rush through it. Take the time to really let it soak in.

❖ **Make the commitment.** Your generation is a busy one, so it is important to set a time on your calendar to meet your mentor, or the meeting will be quickly overtaken by practices and homework. I have provided a covenant for your mentor to have you sign when you start the study. This is not meant to intimidate you, but to motivate you to see this study through until the end. Don't allow distractions to prevent you from the amazing biblical truths that this book discusses.

❖ **Get excited.** God can teach you so much through this if you let Him. I pray that this becomes something that you look forward to every day as God reveals more and more to you.

Now… let's get to work!

A Note To the Mentor: How to Use This Study

If you are the leader reading this, it is an honor for me to pray for you as you walk through this study and teach this generation about the beauty of submission. I pray you will constantly be reminded of what a blessing and honor it is that we have a God who wants to use us and our experiences to change lives. I wanted to share a few notes specifically for you:

❖ **Set a time and place.** Mentoring can take place in a variety of ways and can even occur in a group setting if desired. My experience has shown me that the best thing to do in either situation is to immediately establish a weekly day and time to meet. That way, when schedules get busy the girl(s) already has that time reserved on her calendar.

❖ **Be ready to discuss.** The Bible study itself is directed toward the girl, but in the back of the book there are discussion questions for each section of study for you as the mentor to follow as you walk through it with her. These questions are meant to get the conversation started. As you get to know your "mentee," you will learn which topics need more in-depth discussion than others.

❖ Make sure that the girl or girls understand what is expected of them while taking this study. Don't be unrealistically strict, but give the time spent a level of importance by asking for a bit of sacrifice from them. I have provided a covenant that can be signed by the mentee(s). This covenant also provides a great opportunity for you to talk about those expectations.

Get excited. God can reach people in so many ways, and He allows us to be a part of impacting someone's life. How exciting is that?

Now… let's get to work!

The "I Know I'm Busy but I Really Am Going to Do This" Covenant

Dear Reader,

I want to be up front with you about something: The study that you are about to go through is going to be hard. There are going to be weeks when you are really busy, and distractions come at you constantly. There are going to be weeks when what is asked of you seems like too much. There are going to be weeks when you realize that what this study asks of you doesn't always feel good. There are even going to be weeks when you realize that doing what this study asks of you means you will be running against the tide of where the world is telling you to go.

Can I be honest with you about something else? You can do this. I truly believe that this study will show you how God commands us to live as Christian women, and that He can use us in amazing ways if we allow His Word to soak in. It is worth every ounce of fight you have, and He will give you the strength to follow through. So I challenge you to stick with it and see the ways that God can use you.

Before we start, I ask you to commit to the following:

❖ You will set aside time each day for the next five weeks to do the daily Bible studies in this book.

❖ You will make it a priority to meet with your mentor/Bible study leader once a week for the next five weeks during the time that you schedule.

❖ You will be honest and open during this time and won't be afraid to ask questions so that you can reach for a full understanding of what God is telling you.

❖ You will keep an open mind as you read Scripture about this topic. If there is anything that you struggle with, you will first look at Scripture and then talk with your mentor or Bible study leader.

❖ You will never ever give up.

If you are willing to make these commitments, sign below.

_____

Week One
What Exactly Is This Whole Submission Thing?

Day One: May I Have The Definition Please?

Alright ladies, today is the day that we start our study of this strange topic called submission. Before we begin, if you haven't found an older, Godly woman to meet with during the course of this study, stop and pray about asking someone to join you. This is a deep topic that we are diving into, and although the study is written in such a way that you can do it on your own, I highly encourage you to find someone to go through it with you to help you talk through the difficult parts. Titus 2 gives a great example of why it is important to have a mentor in your life, and guess which topic is used as an example? Yep, submission (vs. 5). This isn't going to be a topic that you intuitively know or are good at, but a Godly woman can help teach you and give you an incredible perspective.

Submission is one of those words that can cause different feelings in the hearts of different people. I remember the first time I really heard the word. I was in middle school, and I was talking with some friends during recess. At one point, a good friend of mine started talking about how her mom was always arguing with her dad because she always wanted to do things differently than him. "My mom said that if my dad just wanted her to shut up and submit to him that that wasn't going to happen," my friend said. "And ya know what? I agree with her! How dare he try and make all the decisions!"

I don't remember much about what happened after that conversation, but I do remember walking away not liking the word submission very much.

What about you? In the space below, write down some thoughts that come to your mind when you hear the word submission:

Let's take a quiz...

Think you already know a lot about this topic? Take a look at some beliefs girls tend to have about submission. Read the following phrases, and circle either "T" for biblically true or "F" for biblically false.

T / F: God commands all believers to submit, not just women.

T / F: True submission to authority means doing as you're told, no matter what, no questions asked.

T / F: God needs us to submit to Him.

T / F: Submission is designed to oppress women because they are not equal to men.

How do you think you did? Let's take a look at these one at a time...

❖ **God commands all believers to submit, not just women.**

TRUE. Did you know that the number one myth about submission is that it only applies to women? Not true! God calls all believers, both men and women, to submit (James 4:7).

❖ **True submission to authority means doing as you're told, no matter what, no questions asked.**

FALSE. As we will see in the next few days, Jesus shows us a great example of what submission looks like. He submitted fully, but made His opinions known in an appropriate way.

❖ **God needs us to submit to Him.**

FALSE. God doesn't ask us to submit because He needs us to. In fact, He can work His plan with or without us (Acts 17:24-25). Instead, His call to submit and trust that He knows what He is doing is for our benefit. He understands that we tend to make life so hard because of sin. If we follow Him, He can give us a life more incredible than anything we could ever ask or think (Ephesians 3:20).

God doesn't just want us to follow a list of rules, He wants to give us an abundant life through following His plan.

❖ **Submission is designed to oppress women because they are not equal to men.**

FALSE. Let me say that again.... FALSE. I could write an entire other book about this misunderstanding. The Bible is clear that both men and women are of equal importance and worth to God. We will soon discover how submission is designed for an incredible purpose where the genders work together, not fight for importance (See Genesis 1:27-28).

So how did you do? Submission is a subject that tends to carry a lot of opinions. Some people hate it. Some people agree with it. Some people speak out against it. Some people think it doesn't apply anymore, and some people just don't know anything about it.

Wherever you land on that spectrum, I want to encourage you to take a few minutes and ask God to help you be open to what His Word might have for you today on this topic.

Since there are so many differing opinions, let's start by laying out a definition of biblical submission.

The word submission is used more than twenty times in the Old and New Testaments. The Greek word used in the New Testament for submission is *hupottasso*. Let's look at that definition...

Hupottasso: To place or rank under, to subject, a voluntary attitude of giving in and cooperating. It is a military term meaning to arrange troops under the command of a leader.[i]

Can I confess something to you? I love all things *Star Wars*. Call me a geek if you want, but when anything related to *Star Wars* comes out in theaters, you can bet that I'll be there (maybe even dressed up as a character!) In case you aren't familiar with it, these sci-fi movies follow a group of "soldiers" known as Jedi who ban together to fight the evils of the Dark Side. One thing that always stands out to me is how much the people training to be Jedi obey the orders of the "masters" who train them. When this leader gives an order, they follow it. In other words, they *submit* to it.

I commonly think of this when I hear the Greek definition of submission. Even though the Jedi trainees don't know everything that is going on, they trust their leader to know what is best for them, so they submit anyway.

Let's take a look at one of the uses of the word *submission* in the Bible, and we can apply this definition to it.

Turn to James 4:7 and write the verse in the space below...

I love this verse because it clearly calls all Christians to submit. There is no room for doubt...submission is a biblical thing for everyone. Let's focus on the first part for right now: *Submit to God.* Now, replace the word "submit" with the Greek definitions...

❖ *Rank or place yourself under* God—Submission is an act of making God the number one boss of our lives. We are to put everything about us second: Our desires, our feelings, our dreams, etc. and follow where He wants us to go.

- ❖ *Subject* yourself to God— Put yourself completely under God's authority. This term is used a lot to describe how a townsperson is subject to their king. A submissive person has the attitude of "what God says goes."

- ❖ *Voluntarily cooperate with* God— I love that this is part of the definition because it shows that true submission cannot be forced. When you truly submit, you do it out of love and trust, not out of fear or because you feel compelled. True submission is when we voluntarily *choose* to follow God.

- ❖ *Arrange yourself under the command of* God—Just like an army trusts its general because he or she has a bigger picture perspective, we can place ourselves under God's authority knowing that He has a plan (more on this tomorrow).

So in the case of James 4:7, we see an example of how we are called to submit to God. As Christians, we submit to God first and foremost, and through our submission to Him we submit to other authorities He places in our lives. We will discuss this in greater depth later on, but with all of this in mind, I have written my version of the definition of submission:

Submission: The act of loving and trusting God so much that we willingly choose to follow Him and the authorities

He places above us because we know that He is worth it.

What do you think about that? These are some pretty intense things that God is asking of us! To not be our own boss? To not make our own decisions? It doesn't sound *anything* like what our culture is telling us as women to do and to be.

> Submission: The act of loving and trusting God so much that we willingly choose to follow Him and the authorities He places above us because we know that He is worth it.

Take a second and write down what is going through your mind right now.

I know this might seem insane, but stick with me. Tomorrow, we are going to look at why we should go along with all of this craziness and submit. As you go throughout your day, I want you to think about what your life would look like if you really did this. Would anything change? Spend some time in prayer, and ask God to speak to you today about what you have learned.

Day Two: Why should I?

Yesterday we looked at a definition of submission and how the Bible clearly states that submission is an important way of life for every Christian (James 4:7). After yesterday's study, you may have been tempted to think, "Ok, I know the Bible says that I should do this…but *why should I?*"

When you were little, do you remember when your parents wouldn't let you do something that you really wanted to do? Once you got a little older, instead of just accepting their authority you probably went through a stage where your first response was, "Why?"

I remember a time in my life when this happened. I was six-years-old and was in the car with my mom. I really wanted to go get some ice cream. I begged and begged, and every time she would say no I would boldly ask, "Why?"

Looking back, I realize that she probably had a million reasons why we couldn't get ice cream that day: It was cold outside, we were in a hurry, my tummy still hurt from all the candy I snuck the night before, etc. However, instead of giving me a reason, she gave the classic parental answer, "Because I said so."

The reality is that God has every right to give us that answer. As believers, when we see that God clearly commands us to do something, we should do it (See James

1:22). But isn't it cool that even though we don't deserve any kind of explanation, there are times when God lovingly gives us one? Praise God that this is one of those times. Today, we are going to look at two other biblical reasons why we should follow this seemingly crazy thing called submission.

1. We submit as a response to what God has done for us.

Open your Bible to Ephesians 2:1-10. Read it over a couple of times. In the space below, write a summary in your own words of what this passage says.

In order to understand the true reason why we should submit, we must first understand the Gospel. If you are unsure of exactly what the Gospel is, take a second to look at the section titled "What is the Gospel?" in the back of this book. Ephesians 2 gives us an amazing example of what God did in our lives through Christ. Let's break it down a little bit.

> In order to understand the true reason why we should submit, we must first understand the Gospel.

Ephesians 2:1-3 talks about who you were before you became a Christian. The descriptions are pretty intense. List them in the space below.

Some of these might be a little tough to understand, so let's look a little deeper:

❖ *You were dead in the trespasses and sins.* Before Christ you were *dead.* No, this isn't talking about a physical death, but a spiritual one. Sin destroyed our capability of having a relationship with God and even our ability to desire one. Because of this, we lived in spiritual darkness, lost and unable to hear from God on our own. God cannot have anything to do with sin, so we were doomed to eternity in a very real place called Hell where we would have been forever separated from Him.

❖ *You were following the prince of the power of the air, the spirit that is now at work in the sons of disobedience.* This talks about how without Christ you are subject to Satan (see also Colossians 1:13 and Galatians 4:3). You may have thought that you were doing your own thing and living your own life, but really you were under the Devil's authority. John 10:10 describes Satan as a thief who wants to steal, kill, and destroy your life. Not only were you following Satan, but you were also actively rebelling against God. That is why this passage refers to those who never give their lives to Christ as "the sons of disobedience."

❖ *You were by nature children of wrath.* Since sin entered our world through Adam and Eve (Genesis 3, Romans 5:12), every single one of us is born against God, and because of this we deserve God's judgment and wrath. If you want an even more descriptive picture of our hopelessness, check out Romans 3:10-20. We do not deserve anything but God's anger.

This probably wasn't the cheery way you wanted to start your day, but before we move on, it is important that we understand this as Christians. Before Christ, you were sinful, lost, and utterly helpless. Not only you, but *everyone* is in this state before they give their lives to Christ. There is nothing you could have done on your own to gain a relationship with God.

The reality is that it could have ended here. God could have left us with what we deserve. Praise Him for Ephesians 2:4-10!

Take a look at those verses again and write down your reaction to this amazing truth.

Even when we were sinful and actively rebelling against God, He sent Christ to die on the cross for our sins to take the punishment that we deserved. Jesus conquered death so that, through Him, we could have a relationship with God, something that we could never earn on our own!

Before we go any further, it is imperative that you stop and ask yourself if you have taken the first step of submission: Have you made God the Boss of your life? Has there been a time in your life that you turned from your sin and believed that Christ is your Savior and the only way to a relationship with God? If you haven't done so, I encourage you to do that today. Talk with your mentor or a pastor. My prayer is that today would be the day that you give your life to Christ!

If you have given your life to Christ, take a moment and reflect on what God has done for you by sending Jesus. Everything we do as believers should be in response to this truth. Submitting to Him in your everyday life is not a way to earn salvation. As you can see from this passage, we are incapable of doing that. Instead, we submit out of thankfulness for the awesome truth that we are saved by His grace alone.

2. We submit because of His great promises.

We have seen that we submit to God because Scripture commands us to and out of a thankful heart for what God has done for us. Lastly, we submit because of His great promises. God gives us dozens of promises throughout Scripture about what He wants to do in our lives when we submit to Him. I've listed some below. Take a few minutes and look them up. Write down the promises they contain in the space next to the verse:

- Jeremiah 29:11

- Hebrews 13:5

- John 10:10

- Ephesians 3:17-21

He promises that He has a plan for our lives. This is a plan that will give us hope and an abundant life that has meaning and joy. He promises that He will never leave us, we can truly know Him, and His plans are so amazing for us that they are beyond what we could ask or think!

With all of this in mind, let's look at our definition for submission again.

Submission: The act of loving and trusting God so much that we willingly choose to follow Him and the authorities He places above us because we know *that He is worth it*.

We have a God that we can trust. We can trust Him when things are good, and we can trust Him when things seem horrible. We can even trust Him by submitting to His commands in our everyday lives. What exactly does that look like? We will explore that tomorrow by looking at how Jesus Himself submitted to God.

Take some time to pray and reflect on what you learned today. In the space below, write what you are thinking thus far.

Day Three: So What Does It Look Like?

The last couple of days we dove right in to this thing called submission. So far, we have looked at what it means to submit, and why we should submit. But what does it look like? How are you supposed to do that in your everyday life? I find no better example of what it looks like to submit than Jesus Christ Himself. He lived His life as a walking, talking example of how God wants us to live our lives. Pull your Bible out and check out Matthew 26. I am going to have the text of the passage written below, but it is really important for you to get out your own Bible and open it up. That way (1) you know that I'm not making this stuff up, and (2) you can look for yourself to see what's going on before and after this passage (AKA the context).

In this passage, we find Jesus in the Garden of Gethsemane just moments before He is going to be arrested to be crucified. We will start at verse 36.

Then Jesus went with them to a place called Gethsemane, and He said to His disciples, "Sit here, while I go over there and pray." And taking with Him Peter and the two sons of Zebedee, He began to be sorrowful and troubled. Then He said to them, "My soul is very sorrowful, even to death; remain here, and watch with Me." And going a little farther He fell on His face and prayed, saying, *"My Father, if it be possible, let this cup pass from Me; nevertheless, not as I will, but as You will."*

Jesus was very distraught because He was fully aware of what was about to happen, and the pain that He was about to endure. He knew that He would not only be beaten and crucified, but also that He would become sin on our behalf in the process. He was so distraught that when Luke wrote of this event, he described Jesus as being in so much agony that He began to sweat drops of blood. Bottom line: Jesus was not excited about what God wanted from Him. But what He does next teaches us three very important steps to submission that can be applied to whomever we are submitting. Don't skim through this part. I will be referring to these steps throughout the rest of this book.

Step 1: Jesus submitted by going to God in prayer (vs.39—*"and going a little farther he fell on his face and prayed"*)

Step 2: Jesus submitted by being honest with God about His desires *("if it be possible, let this cup pass from me")*

Step 3: Jesus submitted to what God decided was best *("nevertheless, not as I will, but as you will.")*

What an incredible example of what submission looks like: Pray, be honest, and submit. We will spend the rest of the week looking closer at these three steps. But today, let's focus on the first one: Jesus submitted by going to God in prayer.

Obviously, this is a very difficult time in Jesus's life. What did Jesus do first when He was overcome with emotion about what God was asking Him to do? Did He consult His closest friends? Did He make a list of pros and cons? Did He read a get-the-best-life-now book? No. He turned to God in prayer.

Prayer is essential in our relationship with God. Even though God knows our heart and our thoughts (see Psalm 139:1-6), prayer is us taking the time to sit before Him and talk to Him. Through prayer we praise Him, thank Him, make requests, and ask Him questions. Feel like you aren't good at it? Don't get caught up in using all the right lingo. Prayer is simply having a conversation with God.

This can be a tough one for us as Christians, but particularly for us as girls. I am definitely a relationally and emotionally-based female, so whenever I have a question in my life, I used to race to the phone or computer to find out which of my friends was available to talk through all the details with me. Often, this would lead to hours of dissecting the problem before coming up with the solution that we thought was best.

Don't get me wrong, it's not a bad thing to consult with a Christian in your life who will give you Godly wisdom, and who is willing to tell you what the Bible says, and not just what they think you want to hear. But, it is important that we talk with these people only *after* we have gone to God in prayer.

The Bible has a lot to say about prayer. Let's take a few minutes and read some of the passages that speak to the point. Read the following passages, and then write in the space next to them what they say about prayer.

❖ Philippians 4:4-7

❖ Psalm 10:17

❖ Psalm 62:8

❖ Hebrews 4:16

As you will see in the rest of this Bible study, prayer is a crucial aspect of submission. Prayer forces us to slow down and talk through an issue with God rather than react based off of our feelings. Since submission can often tug at these emotions, it is important that we go to God first with any decision that we face.

Tomorrow we will look at the second step Jesus used when He was submitting to God. But before we wrap up today, take some time to think through the following questions:

❖ What are some things you need to go to God with today?

❖ How can what you learned today be applied to your everyday life?

Day Four: What Do You Want?

Let's take a look at Matthew 26 again. Yesterday, we started looking at how Jesus is our example when it comes to the "how-to" part of submission. In this passage, we see that Jesus submitted through three steps:

Step 1: Jesus submitted by going to God in prayer.

Step 2: Jesus submitted by being honest with God about His desires.

Step 3: Jesus submitted to what God decided was best.

Yesterday we studied step one and talked about the importance of prayer. Today, let's focus in on step two: Jesus submitted by being honest with God about His desires.

Honesty can be tricky sometimes, especially in the midst of trying to survive high school. I remember so many days when I would go to school and slap a smile on my face just so people wouldn't find out I was struggling or hurting. Do you ever feel like you need to put on a happy face or pretend to be a certain way around people? I know for a lot of girls this can be a big temptation. We put on masks of what we think we are supposed to look and act like, when the reality is we are covering up our thoughts and feelings.

When you read Matthew 26:36-39, one thing is clear: Jesus didn't feel like He had to put a mask on around God. He didn't pretend to be a certain way or act like everything was fine. Jesus was extremely honest with God when He said He did not want to have to go through the agony of the cross. He even went so far as to beg God to change things so He would not have to go through it. Did God get upset? No. Did lightning bolts come from the sky to strike Jesus down? No. God wants you to be honest with Him. He wants you to remove the mask.

One of my favorite examples of this can be found in the book of Psalms. Many of the chapters that you will find written in this book are actually prayers to God from the writer.

> God wants you to be honest with Him. He wants you to remove the mask.

Take a second and check out David's prayer in Psalm 13.

What stands out to you about this Psalm?

What question does the writer ask God (vs. 1)?

Did God really leave him (check out Joshua 1:9)?

Wow. Talk about someone who is honest with God about how he is feeling! David not only told God of his sorrow, but also accused God of leaving him, something that he knew God does not do. But what else did David know? He could be honest with God about how he was feeling.

However, David also knew that our communication with God is not meant to be a mere vent session that ends with us feeling better and getting what we want. Read Psalm 13:5-6 again. David concludes by basically telling God that even though he *feels* neglected, he *knows* in his mind that God is there, and he will trust and worship Him in spite of his feelings.

> Our communication with God is not meant to be a mere vent session that ends with us feeling better and getting what we want.

Now go back to Jesus's prayer in Matthew 26:39. Did He end it with His complaints? No. He ended it with trust in spite of His feelings: "Not as I will, but as You will."

How does this apply to you today? You can be honest with God about your hurts. You can be honest with God about how you feel about that girl who stole your boyfriend. You can be honest with God with how you feel about having to move. You can be honest with God about how you feel about every aspect of your life. However, it is important that in your honesty, you still place your trust in God and submit to Him.

We will tackle the final step of submission tomorrow. Take some time to journal below about what you have learned today. Is there something going on in your life in which you need to be honest with God?

Day Five: Why Submission Isn't for Sissies

The last few days we have been looking at Matthew 26, and how Christ gives us an amazing example of how to submit. Let's look at the steps one more time that we see in verse 39.

Step 1: Jesus submitted by going to God in prayer.

Step 2: Jesus submitted by being honest with God about His desires.

Step 3: Jesus submitted to what God decided was best.

Today, we are going to wrap up this section of our study by looking at step three: Jesus submitted to what God decided was best. In this passage, we have seen Christ pray and beg God to change the events that were about to take place. He pleads with God to the point of blood seeping from his forehead. What was God's response?

He didn't change anything.

This is why I titled the book *Submission Isn't For Sissies*. This is the tough part. Whether you are submitting to God or another authority, there are going to be times when you ask for something and don't get the answer that you want. Maybe your mom still asks for your car keys even though you have a good explanation for why you missed curfew. Maybe you have prayed and prayed to get into a certain college, but you don't get accepted. Or maybe you find out that your family is moving to a new city, and there is nothing you can do to change it.

> Whether you are submitting to God or another authority, there are going to be times when you ask for something and don't get the answer that you want.

Let's be honest, usually our first reaction is to throw a fit. Much like a two-year-old screams in a tantrum, we either yell our anger or we bitterly hold our breath in an attempt to get God to change His mind. If we do choose to submit in a tough situation, we usually do it dragging our feet and grumbling under our breath the entire time. Is this what God wants? Absolutely not. In fact, when God calls us to submit, He asks us to take it a step further: He asks us to do it with *joy*.

Don't throw the book down... stay with me. It's important to remember that submitting does not necessarily mean that you feel happy about it. Jesus submitted to God in this passage, but that didn't mean He suddenly had warm fuzzies about being crucified. Friend, submitting is a choice that often goes against your feelings in that moment. Think back to David in Psalm 13...he clearly was upset about what was going on, but he *chose* to trust and praise God anyway. You may not feel great about it, but submitting means you do what is asked of you...without nagging...without complaining...and without holding a grudge.

> Submitting is a choice that often goes against your feelings in that moment.

A little over a year ago, my husband came home from work with a "we need to talk" look on his face. Once we got the kids tucked into bed, he told me the news: He was up for a promotion that would involve relocating to a new city.

Except for a short time that we lived in a different state, we had lived in Oklahoma City our entire lives. I had a great job that I felt confident in at a church that I loved. We had family just minutes away. We had a beautiful home and the most incredible friendships that I could have ever imagined. Moving meant that I would need to find a new job, a new school for the kids, a new home, and a new church. It would also mean living apart from my husband for months while he started his job, and the kids and I stayed to sell our house. To be honest, I was angry and terrified. How could God remove us from such a great thing?

I remember one day while I was reading a Bible study that I realized that although I was going along with what

God wanted us to do, I wasn't doing it with joy. On that day, I made the decision to not only accept what God called me to submit to, but also to trust God with the plans He had for us even if they didn't line up with my own. Over time, my decision to submit turned into a task that brought me great joy.

Guess what happened? God blessed us in ways that we couldn't possibly imagine.

We talked about this a little bit a few days ago, but take the time to look at these passages again. These are just a few of the promises that God has for us when we trust and submit to Him:

- **Jeremiah 29:11**—He has plans to give you a future and a hope.
- **Hebrews 13:5**— He will never leave you or abandon you.
- **John 10:10**—He has plans that will give you life and life abundant.
- **Ephesians 3:17-21**— We can know Him and He is capable of doing far beyond what we could ask or think.

How do we submit with joy? By trusting and believing in the promises that God has for us. Christ could submit to God with joy even in the toughest of situations because He knew God had a plan. Even though it caused Christ great pain, He knew that it would be worth it to go along with

God's plan. Aren't you glad that He submitted with the decision to die on the cross for us?

Write in the space below something that has happened to you recently that meant you had to submit even though it wasn't what you wanted:

How can you submit *joyfully*?

You can have joy when you don't get into the school you want because you know God has a plan for a future for you. You can have joy when your mom chooses to take away your car keys, or when you find out you have to move to a new place because you know that God's plan cannot be thwarted by any human decision (Job 42:2).

What do you need to pray and ask God to help you submit joyfully to today?

We have looked at what submission is, why we should submit, and what it looks like to submit. Next week we will start looking more specifically at what it looks like to submit to God in our everyday lives.

Week One: Sum It Up!

- ❖ Every believer, whether male or female, is commanded to submit (James 4:7).
- ❖ Submission is the act of loving and trusting God so much that we willingly choose to follow Him and the authorities He places above us because we know that He is worth it.
- ❖ We submit because of the following:
  - ¤ We are commanded to in Scripture.
  - ¤ We are responding to what God has done for us (Ephesians 2:1-10).
- ❖ Because of His great promises (Jeremiah 29:11, Hebrews 13:5, John 10:10, Ephesians 3:17-21).
- ❖ Jesus gives us a powerful example of what submission looks like (Matthew 26:36-39).
  - ¤ He submitted by going to God in prayer.
  - ¤ He submitted by being honest with God about His desires.
  - ¤ He joyfully submitted to what God decided was best.

NOTES

Submission Isn't For Sissies

Week Two
Submit to God

Day One: Remember Who You Submit to First

Crystal[ii], a 17-year-old basketball star, sat in my office weeping. My heart sank as I listened to her describe the events that had taken place over the past few weeks at school. Crystal had met with one of her coaches to tell her that she was going to be missing a basketball game because of a church event. To her surprise, her coach was outraged and benched Crystal for the next two games as punishment. When Crystal approached her, the coach explained that only the truly committed girls get to play on her team, and that she might even bench Crystal the rest of the season. Crystal knew that the coach was not a Christian, but was shocked at this outwardly hateful reaction.

When she was done describing the heart-wrenching events, I couldn't help but ask her the obvious question: "So…what did you do?"

Without hesitation Crystal looked up, and with tears streaming down her face said, "The only thing I could do. I did everything I could to talk highly of my coach to my teammates, encourage her, and to work hard at practice."

I must admit I was so shocked by the answer that I couldn't help but ask, "Why? Why would you do such a thing when she is so horrible to you? She clearly doesn't deserve it!"

It was then that she gave the response that was such a perfect example of true submission: "It doesn't matter if she deserves it or not. I'm not really doing it for her anyway. I'm doing it for God."

Even at a young age Crystal understood that submission to God has to be the root of everything, and that we can't possibly submit to the authorities around us without it. If obeying God and following His commands are not at the heart of your submission, your attempts will be feeble and short-lived.

It is because of this truth that this week we are first going to discover what it means to submit to God. The following two weeks we will look at how we submit to God by submitting to the authorities He puts in place around us. We will then conclude with a week on what it looks like to submit to God by submitting to one another.

> If obeying God and following His commands are not at the heart of your submission, your attempts will be feeble and short-lived.

So how do we submit to God? Take some time to review Matthew 26:36-39. In the space below, write down the "steps" we talked about last week that Jesus used in order to submit to God.

1.

2.

3.

Jesus gives us a perfect picture of what it looks like when we submit to God with our lives. But let's be honest, odds are you aren't going to find yourself in a garden anytime soon sweating blood and pleading for your life like Jesus. So how can you, as a young woman, submit to God in your everyday life? This week we are going to look at four struggles that are common to us as women and explore how we can submit to God with each of them. Why are these things so important? As you look at them, I want you to notice one common theme: If we *don't* choose to submit them to God, they can easily distract us from sharing the Gospel with others.

Think about the last time that you were really worried about something. What was your day like? When you don't like the way you look, are you full of joy and excited to search for people with whom to share Christ? Probably not. Our Enemy loves to distract us, and the topics we are going to talk about are incredible weapons in his tool belt.

Take a moment and look up the following passages. In the space provided, write down what they say about the Enemy that we face.

❖ John 10:10

❖ 1 Peter 5:8

❖ 2 Corinthians 11:3

If we don't choose to submit them to God, they can easily distract us from sharing the Gospel with others.

Scripture says that we have a very real Enemy named Satan who wants to kill and destroy you. He is fully aware that once you become a Christian, he no longer has power over you. However, this father of lies believes that he can silence you by getting you so distracted by the things of this world, that you forget to look around for people who need the Gospel. In summary, he can't touch your salvation, but he can try to shut you up and prevent you from being used to spread the Good News.

Satan longs for us to be consumed with our faults and fears to the point that we are so fixated on ourselves that we don't notice the hurting people around us who need Christ. I want to challenge you to be aware of this trick. Don't let this just be a lesson that you read and then walk away with more head knowledge, but apply these devotionals to your everyday life.

As we close today, take some time to write down some ways that you personally struggle in these areas. Then, take some time to sit in silence, ask God ways you could submit to Him, and write down what comes to your mind. We will start examining these specific topics tomorrow.

1. Submitting to God with my anxieties:

2. Submitting to God with my future:

3. Submitting to God with my circumstances:

4. Submitting to God with my appearance:

Day Two: Submitting to God with Your Anxieties

"What if I never get a boyfriend?"

"What if I don't get into the college I want?"

"What if I don't make the team?"

"What if my Dad loses his job?"

"What if I completely screw up and everyone makes fun of me?"

"What if my parents get divorced?"

Have one or more of the above statements ever run through your head? As girls, we live in a world with a lot of pressure, and it often feels like drama could occur at any moment. The temptation to worry plagues us and often stops us in our tracks.

According to a 2010 study by the Anxiety and Depression Association of America, women are *twice* as likely to suffer from anxiety than men[iii]. Although there are varying opinions as to why that is, the reality is this: Worrying cripples us. Don't forget what we talked about yesterday: It holds us back from the things that God wants us to do, and it silences us from sharing the Gospel with those around us.

It's time to submit to God with our worries.

Like a lot of things in our lives, the above statement is much easier to say than it is to actually do. Like I've said before, this study is not going to be easy, but it is worth the effort. If you are willing to allow God to be the boss and you submit to Him with your worries, you will be able to live a life of incredible freedom in Him.

Let's get started. In the space below, write down some things that tend to cause you to worry.

Now, choose one of those things you listed above, and let's start toward submitting to God with that worry by walking through the steps of submission that Jesus showed us in Matthew 26.

Step 1: Go to God in prayer.

Read Philippians 4:6-7. Write it in the space below.

No matter how big or small you feel your worry is, God wants to hear about it. Take some time and tell God why you're anxious. If you have a hard time audibly speaking the prayer, feel free to write it down and read it to Him. Describe your worries and why they scare you. In a world that tells you that you must be a "tough, independent woman," remember that we have a God who desires for you to be vulnerable with Him.

Read 1 Peter 5:6-9. In the space below, re-write the passage in your own words.

Did you notice the end of verse 7? "casting all your anxieties on Him, *because He cares for you.*" Our God does not look down on you in annoyance toward your anxieties. He desperately wants you to give them all to Him because He loves and cares for you more then you could ever imagine. Satan's number one tactic is to use our fear in casting doubt about God's concern for us. If we doubt that God cares, Satan can inch us toward depression very quickly.

Step 2: Be honest with God about your desires.

What does the above mean in this situation? Tell God what you want! Are you afraid your Dad will lose his job? Tell God that you want your Dad to keep it! Concerned about your future plans? Talk to God about it! Voice these prayers with boldness, telling God the desires of your heart. Remember David in Psalm 13? He didn't hold anything back, and you don't have to either.

However, in the midst of honestly telling Him what you want, don't forget step three.

Step 3: Submit to what God decides is best.

Just like Jesus in the garden, your honesty with God about your desires must be quickly followed with a "but not as I will, as You will" attitude. This means that you trust God so much that, even if you don't get the answer that you want, you will continue to love and serve Him.

I want to teach you an exercise that has really helped me with my worries over the past few years. I will warn you that what I'm going to ask you to think of is going to be really hard for a moment. I want you to think about one of the biggest worries or fears you're facing right now. Now, I want you to think about the worst possible thing that you can imagine happening in that situation. Think about the hurt and the pain that could occur if things don't go the way you would like.

> This means that you trust God so much that, even if you don't get the answer that you want, you will continue to love and serve Him.

Now ask yourself if the worst thing imaginable happened:

Is God still who He says He is?

Are God's promises still true?

Can God still do amazing things "above all that you ask

or think" (Ephesians 3:20)?

Can you still trust Him with every part of your life?

No matter how deep the pain might feel, I want to encourage you by saying that the answer to all of these questions is *yes*. My goal isn't to ruin your day, but I want you to see that even if these horrible things happen, God is *still* everything the Bible says. As you choose to believe the Bible, you will gain so much freedom because your worries will not seem as big anymore.

> As you choose to believe the Bible, you will gain so much freedom because your worries will not seem as big anymore.

Are you struggling with whether the answers to the above questions are really true in your life? Pray and ask God to help you to trust Him. Talk to your mentor or another believer, and let them pray for you and encourage you. Tomorrow we will continue this conversation about worry, but it will be about a very specific kind of worry that many girls face.

Take some time today and read Matthew 6:25-34. Pray that God will give you strength to do what the passage says.

Day Three: Submitting to God with Your Future

Yesterday we started talking about how to submit to God with our worries. Today I want to talk about one anxiety in particular. Working in student ministries has provided many opportunities for me to walk through different situations in girls' lives and teach them how, through Christ, they can conquer anything with which they are struggling. Over the years, I have met with girls about different struggles, but there was one struggle in particular I would have conversations about on a weekly basis.

No, it wasn't sex.

Nope, it wasn't girl drama.

No, it wasn't even struggles with appearance.

The single topic that reared its ugly head time and time again was the overwhelming anxiety about one thing: their future.

I listened and counseled as girls cried in my office because they were afraid they weren't doing enough to get into the college they "needed" to get into. I prayed with them and comforted them as they wept over lost boyfriends, not necessarily because of the boys themselves, but because of the fear that they would wind up alone for the rest of their lives. I watched as the girl with a future in professional athletics suddenly dealt with the staggering reality of an injury. It was in those meetings I discovered that as women we tend to deal with our worry about the future in one of two ways: (1) We submit and find freedom by giving it over to God, or (2) we don't submit and decide He isn't doing a good enough job. So we take it into our own hands to make the future we want for ourselves.

Another way to think about it is that a lot of times we believe the following lie:

If I don't _____, then I will never _____.

If I don't <u>look a certain way,</u> then I will never <u>have a boyfriend.</u>

If I don't <u>cheat on this test,</u> then I will never <u>get into the college I want.</u>

If I don't <u>tear others down so I look the best,</u> then I will never <u>get the career I want.</u>

The list can go on and on. Take a second and think about your future. What lie have you believed? Fill in the blanks with your answer.

If I don't _____, then I will never _____.

Grab your Bible and turn to Genesis 15. Today we are going to take a look at a couple named Abram and Sarai. Together let's look at Sarai's anxiety over her future. Read Genesis 15:1-6.

What was it that Abram so desperately wanted?

What did God promise him?

Abram and Sarai desperately wanted a child, but Sarai was unable to get pregnant. See, in the time that Abram lived, having children was extremely important. Children were the ones whom parents passed everything to and who carried on the family name. The culture held having children in such a high regard that a woman who couldn't get pregnant was considered cursed.

Imagine the relief Sarai must have felt when God told Abram he would have children. However, God's timing was not what Sarai expected. She wanted children right away, and, after years of waiting, she became frustrated and angry at God. She began to believe the lie…

If I don't take control, then I will never have a child.

Instead of trusting God and His timing, we see in chapter 16 that Sarai convinces Abram to be with their servant Hagar, in hopes that Hagar would conceive and give them a son.

This sounds horrible today, but then it was a cultural

norm. However, it is important to note that God never promoted it (see Genesis 2:24). When this happened and Hagar got pregnant, instead of being happy Sarai was overcome by jealousy and caused Hagar to flee.

Did God hold true to His promise? Yes. Sarai did eventually get pregnant and have children. However, there were great consequences for Sarai and Abram's actions toward Hagar. If Sarai had just submitted to God and His timing, centuries of pain and war could have been avoided.

Sarai had a specific promise straight from the Lord that she would have children, and she still tried to take the future into her own hands. The reality is this: God doesn't promise you that you will get married. He doesn't promise you that you will get into the exact college you want, or that you will have the career you thought you would have. He doesn't promise you will one day have children of your own, or that you will win that sports competition. Unlike what the world tells you, He does not promise that if you "follow your heart," you will get everything you want (see Jeremiah 17:9).

But what He *does* promise is that if you submit to Him, He will give you a future full of hope (Jeremiah 29:11) that is abundant (John 10:10) and beyond anything we could ever dream up for ourselves (Ephesians 3:20).

Should you work hard toward your dreams? Absolutely (Colossians 3:23). Should you make plans toward your future? Of course! But don't hold them so tightly that you aren't willing to look around and see that God just might have a better plan than your mind can comprehend. Even if it is painful at first, God will always do much better work than we could ever do ourselves.

As we finish today, pray that God will reveal to you if you have believed the lie that you need to be in control of your future. Tell Him the desires you have for your future, but ask Him to help you joyfully submit to whatever He decides.

> Even if it is painful at first, God will always do much better work than we could ever do ourselves.

Day Four: Submitting to God with Your Circumstances

As women, there really are a lot of things that we have the power to change. For example, with one swift salon purchase we can change the color of our hair in an hour or less. If we decide we are tired of our "look," a trip to the mall can change all of that. Don't like our friends? The reality is that we can change that too. And, let's be honest, we do tend to change our minds quite a bit.

I wonder if we love to change things because it makes us feel more in control. I love to feel like I have control of the things that are going on around me. However, the reality is that we have *no* control over so many things.

This is especially true when it comes to most of the circumstances we face in our lives. For example, we can't change if we are born to parents who love us or to parents who don't care about us. We have no control over if we are born in a country filled with oppression and poverty or a country filled with opportunity. We have no control if we are perfectly healthy or if we have disabilities or illnesses that plague us our entire lives. I could list many examples of circumstances that are extremely difficult, and yet there is nothing that can be done to change them.

Today, let's look at a story about when the disciples felt a lack of control. Grab your Bible and read Luke 8:22-25. In the space below, write down what happens in this story.

In this passage, the disciples weren't excited about their circumstances. They were tired after working a long day, and instead of getting rest, they were scrambling around trying to keep their boat afloat during a massive storm.

When they realized they couldn't stop the storm, to whom did they run?

What was Jesus doing?

Were the disciples irritated when they discovered that Jesus was sleeping? Absolutely. They had been desperate for a solution to their troubles, and here they find the King of Kings taking a cat nap. When we have difficult circumstances in our lives, it can be easy to feel frustrated at God. Maybe you have had days where, like David, you want to scream at the top of your lungs, "How long will you forsake me?" (Remember Psalm 13 from last week?) Or maybe there are just days where you feel like God must be sleeping instead of caring about what you're going through (check out Psalm 121:3-4).

What does Jesus do when He wakes up?

Jesus wasn't sleeping because He didn't care. He was fully aware of what was going on. He was sleeping to demonstrate that He wasn't freaking out because He was in control. So much control, He could stop the wind and the waves in an instant (Isaiah 26:3).

> When we have difficult circumstances in our lives, it can be easy to feel frustrated at God.

Today I want to encourage you that no matter what you face, you can submit to God with your circumstances because He is in control.

For some of you, the reminder that God is in control is a big comfort. For others, those words might cause pain in your heart upon first glance. If God is in control, does that mean that He is allowing horrible things to happen to me? Yes. If God is in control, does that mean He can put a stop to the storm I'm going through, yet He is choosing not to? Yes. This can be a hard reality with which to deal.

Before you let the pain and hurt take over, let's remember some specific things about our circumstances.

1. God's desire was for us to live in a perfect world without pain.

Genesis describes a world that God created where there was no pain, tears, or toil. It was a world free of sin where God and mankind could literally walk together in perfect communion. However, God didn't want us to be robots devoid of choice. So He devised a test. He placed one tree in the garden and told them not to eat from it. That way, if man ate from it, they would be choosing to disobey God.

When Adam and Eve made the choice to eat from the tree, sin came in and caused the perfect world God had created to crumble. Now we live in a world where there is much pain, much toil, and many tears because of that sin. Praise God that He sent Jesus so that when He returns we can one day experience a world without sin! Take a look at Genesis 2-3 for all the details.

2. Even in a world of sin and painful circumstances, God promises that He can take all things and use them for the good of those who belong to Him (Romans 8:28).

He can take the hard thing that you're going through and use it to strengthen you, and to help you bring glory to Him (James 1:2-4). Even if you are caught up in a circumstance because of a bad choice you made, you can trust in God and allow Him to take control.

So how do you deal with the times in your life that *feel* terrible and never-ending? You can either allow the pain to consume you, or you can submit to God and choose to trust that He is in control even in the most raging storms that you face.

As we close today, I want to take a look at a man in the Bible who had some really hard circumstances that were out of his control, and yet He submitted to God in the midst of them.

Look up Job 1 and read verses 1-5. In the space below, write what you learn about Job in this passage.

Job was a man who trusted God and who was extremely wealthy. He had a wife and many children whom he loved very much. He was incredibly blessed.

Now let's read the rest of the story. Take some time and read the rest of Job 1. Make a list of the circumstances Job dealt with in the space below.

When all of this was finished and Job was in immense grief, what did he do (vs. 21-22)?

What did Job *not* do?

If you continue to read in Job, you will see that he is struck with terrible health issues and has to deal with immense amounts of pain every day. Yet even when his wife and friends question God, Job stays faithful and submits his circumstances to God. In the end, God blesses him greatly and rebuilds all that Job had lost.

The point of the story isn't that Job was faithful so that God would give him lots of stuff in the end. The reality is that you can submit to God in your circumstances, and He might still choose not to change them. However, you will

> The reality is that you can submit to God in your circumstances, and He might still choose not to change them. However, you will be blessed by trusting God. He will never let you down, and He is always faithful even when you are faced with circumstances that are beyond your control.

be blessed by trusting God. He will never let you down, and He is always faithful even when you are faced with circumstances that are beyond your control.

Take some time today and go find a quiet place where you can sit and talk with God. Pray and be honest about how your circumstances make you feel and tell Him your desires. Ask Him to help you to submit your circumstances completely to Him.

Day Five: Submitting to God with your Appearance

Take some time and pray before we begin today's topic: Submitting to God with your appearance. Ask God to open your heart as you read His Word today. Ask that it would cause a change in your life.

There's no question that insecurities are a huge struggle for us as women. Whether it be our weight, height, nose, complexion, voice, etc., all of us can quickly find something that we don't like about our appearance. In her book, *Graffiti: Learning to See the Art in Ourselves,* Erin Davis reveals some startling statistics about women and their insecurities with how they look:

- ❖ More than half of females surveyed between the ages of eighteen and twenty-five would rather be run over by a truck than be fat. Two-thirds of women in that age group would choose to be mean or stupid rather than be fat.

- ❖ The number one wish for females ages eleven to seventeen is to lose weight.

- ❖ There has been a rise in incidents of anorexia in fifteen to nineteen-year-olds every year since 1930.[iv]

And why wouldn't we have a skewed vision of beauty? Let's face it, we live in a world that is all about outward appearance. The world tells us that we were born with flaws that need to be fixed, and that we are defined by what we look like. But God's Word paints for us a completely different picture.

Read what the following verses have to say about your appearance. In the space provided, write the verses out in your own words.

- Psalm 139:14

- Ephesians 2:10

- 1 Timothy 2:9

- 1 Samuel 16:7

- 1 Peter 3:3-4

The Bible repeatedly reminds us as men and women that God created us the way we are, and that He has a plan and a purpose for the way that we look. Not only that, but He created us in His own image(Genesis 1:27)! Yet so often we fall into the lie that we need to change the way God made us because the world doesn't think it's good enough.

I remember when I was in high school, and I went through an intense time of struggle with how I looked. I went to a girl's retreat where they told me about the verses above. They told me to just repeat those passages to myself constantly, and that eventually I would be happy with my looks. I did what they said, but instead of feeling freedom, I only found more struggle and frustration. The Bible verses didn't stop the girl from my third hour class from making fun of me every day. The Bible verses didn't stop that boy I liked from dating my friend simply because she had better curves than I did. The Bible verses didn't stop the pain I felt.

It took some time, but God in His mercy gently taught me why it wasn't working. Even though I was reading those Bible verses, I was continuing to dwell on my appearance instead of fully submitting and trusting God with the way He made me. Instead of just reading Psalm 139, I needed to choose to believe it. Did it stop the teasing or that boy from dating my friend instead of me? No. Even the Bible says that the world is all about looks (1 Samuel 16:7). That reality is not going to change. But slowly it can look like this...

> Instead of just reading Psalm 139, I needed to choose to believe it.

"God, I don't like the way I look, but I know You made

me this way on purpose so I will choose to go with confidence today because I trust You."

"God, I'm sad that boy doesn't like me because of my looks, but I know You have a plan for me so I will choose to trust You with my dating life."

"God, that girl keeps teasing me, but I know You gave me these qualities and You think they are perfect. So I'm going to choose to believe You instead of letting her distract me from the plan You have for me."

What would your thoughts look like if you really submitted to what the Bible says about your looks? Write some thoughts in the space below.

God has a plan for your life, even for your looks. When I was younger, I overheard two guys talking about a girl at their school. They were talking about how hot she was, and how they wished that they could get a date with her. I listened in, and after a few moments asked them if they thought that I was hot. The answer I got? "Well, Kelly, you're pretty, but you're only pretty if you have makeup on. Truly hot girls don't need makeup to be beautiful."

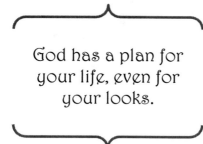

God has a plan for your life, even for your looks.

Can you guess what I did? I spent the next few years of my life refusing to go out in public without makeup on.

Last year I went to a marriage conference with my husband of six years. At the conference the speakers told the spouses in the room to turn to one another and tell the other person what one of the first things was that attracted you to him or her. Can you guess what my husband said to me? He said, "One of the things that truly attracted me to you was that you don't need makeup to be pretty. You are absolutely beautiful *without* your makeup on." Can you believe it? I spent so much time focused on not thinking I was pretty because of what those boys said, yet the entire time God knew that He had a man chosen for me to be my husband who would find me beautiful without my makeup on!

That day I learned that when God says He has a plan for someone's life, that includes how that person looks. Submit to Him today. Pray the words of Psalm 139 out loud to Him today. Trust Him with your looks. Why? Because when you find your confidence in Christ, He can use you to do incredible works for His kingdom. The Enemy knows that he can keep you silent by making you feel insecure. You must battle back by submitting to God and choosing to trust Him with how He made you. Today, when you look in a mirror, choose to thank God that He has a plan for how He made you.

Week Two: Sum It Up!

- ❖ We can apply the same steps Jesus used to submit in Matthew 26 in order to submit to God the things we struggle within our daily lives.
- ❖ We have a very real Enemy who wants to use the struggles we have to silence us when it comes to sharing the Gospel with others.
- ❖ We can submit to God with our *anxieties* by understanding that even in the worst of circumstances, He is still who He says He is, and His promises are still true.
- ❖ We can submit to God with our *future* by trusting that He has plans that are far beyond what we could ever ask or think (Ephesians 3:20).
- ❖ We can submit to God with our *circumstances* by knowing that He is in control.
- ❖ We can submit to God with our *appearance* by embracing the fact that He has created us the way we are for a reason.

NOTES

Kelly Wehunt

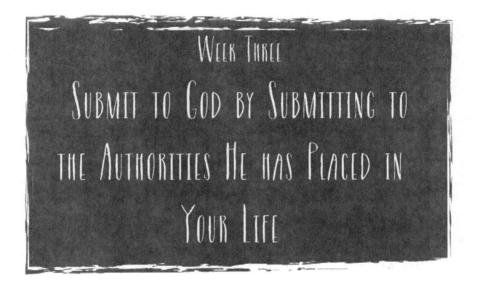

Week Three

Submit to God by Submitting to the Authorities He has Placed in Your Life

Day One: God Has Placed Authority Over You

We have covered a lot over the past couple of weeks! My prayer is that this study has challenged you with this beautiful yet difficult topic of submission. So far, we have talked about what submission is and how to submit to God with some difficult things that we as women face. Over the next two weeks, we will take on the next challenge when it comes to submission: Submitting to God by submitting to the authorities that He has placed in our lives.

Authority? You mean the people that think they are "in charge" of me? I know that just the thought makes some of you shudder in the same way that it used to make me.

Let's be honest… teenage girls are not necessarily known for obeying authority. If you ask a person to describe teenagers in general, a word that most likely will pop up is "rebellious." Why? Because for the first time in your life your brain has gotten to a point where you start developing your own ideals and ideas. Gone are the days of doing what your parents want just because they say "because I said so." Now you want answers. You want to know *why* you're being asked to do something, and if it isn't a good enough answer, you are tempted to rebel and go in the direction *you* think is best.

How do you feel about authority? Take some time to write down your thoughts.

Today we will talk about one specific truth that is so important for us to understand when it comes to the struggles we have submitting in this area: God is the one who has placed authority over you.

Open your Bible to 1 Peter 2:13-17. In the space below, summarize what the passage says in your own words.

This is just one of many examples of God calling believers to submit to human authorities. Notice in verse 14 it talks about the governors "sent by Him." We are called to submit to these human authorities because God is the one who put them into place (also see Romans 13:1, Colossians 1:16, and Daniel 2:21).

This means that no one is in authority without God allowing it. Now if you have seen the news at any time in the last few years, you're probably thinking of some pretty vile authorities you have seen in different parts of the world. Or maybe you look at how your teacher treats you or even the terrible ways your parents treat you. Or you might be in a situation, like Crystal, where a coach is treating you unfairly. Why would God allow those men and women to be in positions of authority? We will dig into that question more deeply tomorrow, but the important thing to remember today is that we have a God who is completely in control, which means the authorities we deal with are put in place by Him.

> We are called to submit to these human authorities because God is the one who put them into place.

Now, let's take a closer look at the end of our passage in 1 Peter 2. Read verse 16 again.

Live as people who are free, not using your freedom as a cover-up for evil, but living as servants of God.

What do you think this verse means? Read it a few times slowly before writing in the space below.

It's interesting how often people twist submission into this horrible thing that takes away our freedom. Yet, in this verse, we are encouraged to live as free people, but not to use our freedom as a way to cover up evil. What does that mean? Just because you're a Christian and you don't agree with an authority doesn't mean you can use your freedom in Christ as an excuse to treat that authority with no respect. Why? God is the one who places authority over you. It wasn't an accident. It does have a purpose.

> Just because you're a Christian and you don't agree with an authority doesn't mean you can use your freedom in Christ as an excuse to treat that authority with no respect.

So who are these authorities that God has put in our lives? Let's take a look at Scripture and make a list.

❖ Read 1 Peter 2:13-18

This passage speaks of two different authorities in which to submit. What is the first one?

This passage first speaks directly about submitting to the government and law enforcement. We see this echoed in Romans 13:1-7 as well as in other passages.

What is the second authority mentioned (take a look at vs. 18)?

This passage tells slaves to submit to their masters. We will discuss in depth why the Bible talks about slavery next week, but I believe biblically this call to submit covers the categories of employees submitting to their employers, students submitting to their teachers, and athletes submitting to their coaches.

❖ Read Ephesians 6:1-3.

To what authority does this passage call us to submit?

This authority is also mentioned specifically as one of the Ten Commandments. Check out Exodus 20:12. Why do you think that this authority is held to such a high importance?

❖ Read Hebrews 13:17.

Who are the leaders that you are asked to obey? (Hint: Read Hebrews 13:7. What leader speaks the Word of God to you? Acts 20:28 also mentions these overseers of the church.)

❖ Read Ephesians 5:22-33

Who does God call us as women to submit to in this passage?

Typically, when people think of submission, this verse is what immediately comes to mind. Next week we will see the importance of this one, and how it even applies to single women.

Let's make a list of these authorities. As Christians, we are commanded to submit to the following authorities God has placed in our lives:

1. _____ (1 Peter 2:13-17)

2. _____, _____, _____ (1 Peter 2:18)

3. _____ (Ephesians 6:1-3)

4. _____ (Hebrews 13:17)

5. _____ (Ephesians 5:22-33)

Wow, that's a pretty big list of authorities God has put into place. Take some time to look over these different categories of authorities. Do any of them surprise you? To which ones are the most difficult to submit? Make notes with thoughts, questions, or struggles that come to mind as you pray over each one. Tomorrow we will look into why we should submit to these authorities God has put into place.

Day Two: But They Don't Deserve It!

Yesterday, we created a pretty hefty list of authorities to which God asks us to submit. I remember the first time someone talked to me about submission, and how God commands us to obey human authorities that are placed over us. I remember being really overwhelmed, and I went through a few weeks where one question lingered in my mind...

Why?

If I am submitting to God, isn't that enough? Why should I have to mess with obeying such imperfect and often undeserving authorities as well?

It is absolutely true that there are going to be times when someone does not deserve your submission. Here are four important things to keep in mind when it comes to the authorities that are in place in your life:

1. God has allowed that person to be in authority.

We laid this foundation yesterday, but it is so important for us to remember. This means that there is no person in authority in your life who slipped into place without God noticing. We have a God who sees and who has interest in every detail. He is fully aware of who that authority is and how they are behaving. This brings us to the next point.

2. Just because God allows a person to be in authority does not mean God approves of what they are doing.

We live in a world full of sin, and all people have sinned (Romans 3:23). It is important to note that just because an authority has been instituted by God, it does not mean that the authority is Godly or perfect in their actions.

In Scripture, we see several examples of God allowing a person to be in authority even though God did not approve of what they are doing. King Saul tried to kill David on numerous occasions (1 Samuel 19), King Nebuchadnezzar tried to get everyone to worship him instead of God (Daniel 3), and King Herod even tried to have baby Jesus killed (Matthew 2). These men did things that were so wicked that Christians could *not* submit to them (more on this later). Yet God still allowed them to be in authority. This is where the next point is really important to understand…

> Just because an authority has been instituted by God, it does not mean that the authority is Godly or perfect in their actions.

3. God will hold everyone in authority accountable for their actions.

Take a look at Hebrews 13:17. Write it in your own words below.

This particular passage speaks specifically about submitting to the authorities God has placed in your church, but it is a concept that is applied to all authorities in your life: They will be held accountable for how they lead (James 3:1.) The people God places in authority are held to a higher standard of accountability and will feel the consequences of their actions (that means one day when you are in a position of authority, *you* will be held accountable too.) So why is it important for you to know this? **Because it's not your job to judge the authorities in your life. It is your job to submit to them.** No authority can mess up the plan that God has for your life. No authority can take away the promises that God has made you. Trust God and submit.

4. When you submit to your authorities, you are really submitting to God.

When you are dealing with a problematic authority and you feel overwhelmed and fed up because you know they don't deserve your obedience, remember they don't deserve it, *but God does.*

It might be an authority

> No authority can mess up the plan that God has for your life. No authority can take away the promises that God has made you. Trust God and submit.

that doesn't give you the respect you deserve...but God gives you a kind of love you could never earn.

It might be an authority that makes you think you are worthless. But God thinks you are worth everything, even sending Jesus to die so you can have a relationship with Him.

It might be an authority that is trying to ruin all your plans...but God has a plan for you that can never be ruined (Jeremiah 29:11) and is more amazing than you can even imagine (Ephesians 3:20).

It might be an authority that always lets you down, but God will never let you down.

Today, look at the four things listed above. Think about them and allow God to speak to you. That authority you struggle with may not ever be "worthy" of your submission. But God is, so thank Him for being so worthy today.

Day Three: But I Really Really Really Don't Agree!

Yesterday, we talked about how we must submit to the authorities that are placed in our lives because God is the one who put them there. In yesterday's time of study, I put forth a very blunt statement that I want you to think about again today:

It's not your job to judge the authorities in your life. It is your job to submit to them.

So... wait a second, Kelly... are you saying that it is wrong for me to question the authorities in my life if they are doing something wrong? That if I see an injustice happening, I should just be silent? Are you saying that all of those women who fought for equal rights were sinful in doing so, or that slaves were wrong for fighting for freedom?

Absolutely not. When those groups fought for rights in a biblically correct way, they were right to do so.

Remember the three steps of submission that we learned from Jesus in the Garden of Gethsemane? Write them below (glance back at Week One, Day Four):

1.

2.

3.

Now, write these same steps but how they apply when we submit to the authorities around us.

God gives us a voice and, as believers, we should always stand up for the biblical rights of others. This is one of those areas where it is crucial that your foundation is rooted in God's Word. It can be easy to be persuaded by what "feels right" to you at the time, but what does the Bible really say? If there is a situation that, after much prayer, you decide to speak up, do so in a loving and respectful way.

Is it possible to disagree with someone in a loving way? Absolutely!

According to James 1:19, how might one respectfully disagree with another?

Most likely, your temptation is going to be to skip praying and say what is on your mind in the moment. Stop and pray. I always recommend that you wait until at least the next day, if possible. Also realize that, as you pray, God might tell you just to submit and not disagree. Trust and obey what He says.

Now read James 1:26 and James 3:8-12. What do these verses reveal to us?

Girls, this is a tough one. The number one way for you to be *dis*-respectful and *un*-loving when approaching an authority with a disagreement is for you to first go and gossip to all of your friends about the situation. Gossip not only shows a non-submissive heart, but also, your friends are not going to encourage you to submit to the authority. They will bash him or her along with you in order to be a "good" friend and make you feel better. The last thing you want to do when approaching an authority is to gang up on him or her and casually mention that you've talked to others. Don't stir up drama. No gossip. Not even "venting."

> Gossip not only shows a non-submissive heart, but also, your friends are not going to encourage you to submit to the authority. They will bash him or her along with you in order to be a "good" friend and make you feel better.

Now read Ephesians 4:25-27 and write down what it reveals to us about disagreements.

Set up a time and a place where you can talk face to face privately. Let me reiterate— *face to face*. A disagreement should *never* take place over text-messaging, social media, or on the phone. If a face-to-face meeting makes you nervous, write down what you want to say beforehand and take it with you to read to the person. So much can be misinterpreted when read on a text message or listened to on the phone without seeing facial expressions. All of that can be avoided by meeting face-to-face.

Last but not least, check out Matthew 26:39. Write down what it says in your own words.

Don't forget, Jesus told God what He wanted, but He did so in a way that expressed that He would do whatever God decided in the end. No matter how unfair the situation might seem, we are still called to submit to what the authority decides. Why? God will hold that authority accountable for how they lead. It is not your job to judge or punish them. It is your job to submit. When talking to an authority about a disagreement you have with a decision, make sure that you express that you understand that their decision is final. This keeps the conversation from sounding threatening and keeps it under the umbrella of "I'm letting you know my thoughts, but I recognize that you are the one in control." Also, remember that part of showing respect to an authority is exhibited by asking the authority for permission to express your concerns.

Are there ever times to not submit? Actually, the answer is yes. These are rare situations, but they are important for you to understand. Tomorrow we will take a look at these circumstances and how to handle them. Today, take some time to pray over how you treat the authorities in your life. Have you ever disagreed with someone in a disrespectful way? God may be calling you to go and apologize to that authority. Ask that God would show you if you have been disrespectful and how He would have you deal with that situation.

Day Four: When It's Time to Say No

Once, long ago, there were three men who lived in a land ruled by an egotistical and often insane king. One day, that king had some of his subjects construct a giant, golden statue of himself and place it in the middle of the city. He declared that every day when the townspeople heard the trumpets, they must immediately bow down and worship this statue. He even decreed that if anyone refused to submit to his laws, they would be thrown into a fiery furnace.

Does this story sound familiar? If you have never read the story of these three men (Shadrach, Meshach, and Abednego), be sure and take some time to read it in Daniel 3 today. These men were faced with a decision as to whether or not to submit to their authority. In this case, they chose not to, and God approved of that choice.

Today, we are going to look at two occasions when you should not submit to an authority that God has allowed in your life. Before we begin, let's make something clear: These are going to be rare occasions in your life. I am not providing this list so you can look for a loophole to avoid submission. However, when faced with a choice to submit, it is important to understand that the Bible does provide examples of when submitting to an authority is wrong.

1. You should never submit to an authority in a situation where they are asking you to go against what the Bible says, resulting in sin.

Shadrach, Meshach, and Abednego knew not to submit to the king because he was asking them to go against one of God's commandments: To have no other gods but God (Exodus 20:3-5).

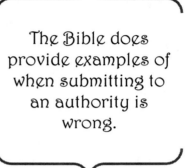

The Bible does provide examples of when submitting to an authority is wrong.

A great place to look at what the Bible says about sin is the Ten Commandments. These were commandments God gave to us as specific and clear ways to understand what is sinful and what is not. It is so important to study these and other Old Testament writings because they show us what sin is, what the consequences of sin are, and how badly we need a Savior.

Read Exodus 20:1-17. Let's take a look at each commandment and discover how to decide whether or not to submit.

Commandments 1 & 2

❖ Read Exodus 20:3-6.

The first two commandments speak directly about keeping God first in your life, and worshipping no other gods but God. This means if you have an authority that is telling you to worship something other than God or telling you to say that God isn't real, you are not to submit to that authority in that situation.

Keep in mind that if you have an authority that requires you to spend a majority of your time doing something other than worshipping or serving God, you still submit to that authority. For example, if your parents force you to sign up for a sports team or get a job that requires time away from church a lot, it would be wrong to tell them no even though church is an important part of a Christian's life. Pray and discuss your reasons for wanting to make church a higher priority and ultimately still submit.

Commandment 3

❖ Read Exodus 20:7.

This commandment tells us that we should always use God's name in a respectful and thoughtful way. If you aren't talking *about* God or talking *to* God, it isn't an appropriate time to use His name. You should never submit to an authority in a situation where they are requiring you to use words like "God," "Jesus Christ," "Lord," etc. in a disrespectful way. Scripture is very clear that we will be held accountable for every careless word we speak (Matthew 12:36-37).

If you have an authority that breaks this commandment and does use God's name in careless ways, this does not release you from submitting to them as long as they aren't asking you to do the same thing.

Commandment 4

❖ Read Exodus 20:8-11.

It is important to not get so busy that we neglect to spend time with God. You should not submit to an authority in a situation where they are never allowing you to have time with God. We see an example of this through the multiple missions organizations that support underground churches and provide Bibles to people who live in countries where the government does not allow them.

If your parents do not allow you to attend church, this does not mean that you can sneak out and go anyway. This is a tough one, but while you are under their roof you can show great love and respect to them by honoring their wishes if they tell you not to attend church. Choose wisely, but look for times to get into calm, non-fighting conversations about the issue. A close friend of mine encountered that situation when he was younger. He stayed in contact with a youth pastor at a local church who would check on him and send him Bible studies, but he waited until his stepdad approved before he actually attended church. This act of respect spoke loudly about Christ's love to his stepdad.

Commandment 5
❖ Read Exodus 20:12.

God specifically appointed your parents to a position of authority. Why? Because if you can learn to submit to your parents—the people who you live with and are around all the time—you have amazing practice for submitting to the other authorities God puts in your life. If any authority tells you to do something that goes against your parents, you should not submit to them.

If your parents are asking you to do something contrary to the other Ten Commandments, or if they are treating you in a way that is abusive (we will talk about that in a moment), ask for guidance from a pastor or a Godly influence that you trust.

Commandments 6-10
❖ Read Exodus 20:13-17.

These commandments are pretty straight forward. If anyone asks you to do any of these things, do not submit. Keep in mind that adultery includes looking at pornography (Matthew 5:28) and that murder includes hating someone (1 John 3:15).

If you are in a situation where you are being asked by an authority to do any of these things, practice the first two steps of submission: Pray and respectfully voice why you cannot do what they are asking. If they give you no choice and insist on your compliance, then in the words of the apostle Peter, you "must obey God rather than men" (Acts 5:29), knowing that the consequences may be unpleasant. You may have to accept the loss of a job, the loss of a place on the team, or the loss of a relationship. But no matter what happens, know that God's promises are still true, and He is with you when you go through those trials.

As we have seen, you should never submit to an authority who is trying to make you sin. Now, let's look at the other permissible reason to not submit to an authority.

2. Never submit to an authority if what they are doing/asking you to do is physically or psychologically harmful.

If you have an authority in your life who is abusing you in any way, you need to immediately go to a pastor, teacher, or counselor you trust for guidance. There is no excuse for this kind of behavior, and it is not your fault it's happening.

If you think you are being abused and have a question about it, talk to someone. *Do this even if that authority has told you not to tell anyone.*

These are situations that are difficult, but it is extremely important to be prepared in case they happen. Keep in mind that just because you don't feel great about something you are asked to do, it doesn't necessarily mean that it is something to which you shouldn't submit. It is always important to compare the situation to Scripture, and if you still aren't sure, talk to a Godly mentor who will be honest with you. Take some time today and pray about what you are submitting to right now. Ask God to give you strength to continue to submit and to have wisdom if faced with a tough situation.

Day Five: Submitting for the Sake of the Gospel

Remember at the beginning of last week when I told you the story of Crystal and how she was being treated unfairly by her coach? Crystal knew that her coach's choice to sit her on the bench was unfair. After much prayer, Crystal approached her coach one day after school to talk to her about it. She explained to her coach that she had put a lot of effort into the team, and that she didn't feel it was right to be punished just because she missed one game for a church event. She ended the conversation with the statement: "I feel you are treating me unfairly. However, you are my coach, so I will submit to whatever you decide."

In my mind, Crystal could not have handled that situation any better. She did everything right by going straight to her coach and talking to her directly about the situation. But we know the end of the story. Even though Crystal did everything right, her coach still benched her for the rest of the season. What did Crystal do? She kept her word and submitted to her coach's decision.

At the time, it seemed like a horrific circumstance to Crystal. After all, she had worked hard her entire life in order to play basketball, and this one authority was doing something that could take it all away. But Crystal understood that her life was not about being a basketball player, it was about something bigger.

> It shows people what Christianity truly is: Giving up your own life and desires and letting God take the lead.

Read 1 Peter 2:13-17. In the space below, write down what the passage says about why you should submit to authorities.

Now read 1 Peter 3:1-2. We'll look at this passage more when we discuss submitting to husbands next week, but why does this passage say wives should submit to their husbands?

Do you see a pattern? Your submission points others to Christ! Why? Because it is so radical and so crazy in the world's eyes that, when you do it, people take notice. Not only that, it shows people what Christianity truly is: Giving up your own life and desires and letting God take the lead. Your submission is the perfect illustration of this spiritual truth.

Instead of running away, God called Crystal to stay and submit. Crystal obeyed, and God used that tough year in her life to teach her so many things. Crystal continued to show love to her coach and refused to gossip about her. After much prayer, she decided to stay on the basketball team anyway, hoping for more opportunities to share Christ with her coach. She got those opportunities, including a time when she was able to share the Gospel because her coach was so shocked at how this teenage girl treated her in spite of sitting her on the bench.

We have two choices when it comes to authorities that seem unfair in our lives. We can share our opinion in a respectful way but still submit to what is decided, or we can throw a tantrum, gossip, cut down, and rebel against the authority. This could squash any chance we have at sharing the Gospel with that person.

And let's be honest, gossiping, talking badly, and rebelling are much easier to do than submitting. So easy, that most people will choose that path.

Read Matthew 5:43-47 in your Bible. Write down what it says in your own words.

In this passage, Jesus is challenging Christians who aren't treating the enemies in their lives with love. Pay careful attention to vs. 46-47. Notice how He calls out Christians, saying that even people who don't know Him (referred to in this passage as tax collectors and Gentiles) love their friends. If you want to look different than the rest of the world, you must take the more difficult path and love people who are horrible to you and don't deserve it (your enemies).

The same applies to submission. It's easy to submit to an authority that you agree with or who is asking you to do easy things. Even people who don't know Christ do that. Want to stand out? Submit to authorities who are difficult, and who ask you to do things you don't necessarily want to do.

I did a lot of different things in high school. I had a lot of friends, I played sports, I went to youth group and school dances. Even though I had some hard times, overall I had a blast. But do you know what's funny? Now that I'm older and think back on high school, my mind doesn't automatically go to those moments. Instead, I find joy looking at the times that I got to share the Gospel with my friends and especially the times that I got to see their lives change forever by making Jesus the authority of their lives.

Let's look at one more example in Scripture of someone who understood that submission could show people the Gospel. Read Acts 16:22-33. Write a list of events that occur in this passage.

Did you catch it? Paul and Silas were beaten and thrown into prison for sharing the Gospel with those around them. But when God sent an earthquake that opened up their jail cells what did they do? Nothing. See, back then, if a jailer lost one of his prisoners, he would be executed in his or her place. So when the jailer saw that the cells had opened, he attempted to take his own life. Did Paul and Silas have the opportunity to run away? Yes. But instead, they trusted God and stayed in their cell. This act of submission resulted in the jailer receiving Christ that day.

In the midst of the hardships that submission can bring, don't forget the impact you can have on someone's life. The dates, dances, and pep rallies will all fade away, but you will never forget the life change in which God allows you to be a part.

As we end this week, read Colossians 3:23. I want to encourage you to write it down and put it in a place where you will see it as we continue our study. We will be diving deeper into these different authorities in which God has called us to submit to and how to deal with the specific challenges each of them bring. Pray that He prepares your heart for areas of your life in which you need to fully trust Him.

Week Three: Sum it Up!

- ❖ The human authorities that God has put in our lives include:
    - ¤ Government/Law Enforcement (1 Peter 2:13-17)
    - ¤ Teachers, Employers, and Coaches (1 Peter 2:18)
    - ¤ Parents (Ephesians 6:1-3, Exodus 20:12)
    - ¤ Church Leaders (Hebrews 13:17)
    - ¤ Husbands (Ephesians 5:22-33)
- ❖ Just because God allows an authority to be in place does not mean that He approves of what they are doing (Romans 13:1, Colossians 1:16).
- ❖ We can respectfully disagree with an authority by following the same steps Jesus did in Matthew 26:
    - ¤ Pray and ask God what to do in the situation.
    - ¤ Go and tell the authority your desire in the situation.
    - ¤ Ultimately, submit to what the authority decides.
- ❖ There are times when you should not submit to an authority.
    - ❖ Submission can open a doorway for you to share the Gospel with those around you.

Kelly Wehunt

NOTES

Submission Isn't For Sissies

Week Four
All These Authorities... How Do I Submit to Them?

Day One: "Children, Obey Your Parents"

I was outraged. I couldn't believe what was happening. Didn't they trust me? Didn't they care about me and my social life? Didn't they understand that I was seventeen-years-old? No matter what I did or how many reasonable arguments I came up with, one thing remained the same: My parents were the reason that I was the *only* senior with a 10 p.m. curfew.

When the word "parents" comes to your mind, some of you immediately think of situations like mine. Others can think of even worse situations when your parents imposed a rule that hurt you badly. Regardless of your relationship with your parents, the Bible is extremely clear about one thing: Submitting to them is a big deal to God.

Let's take a closer look at a few of the passages where this is directly addressed. In the space provided, write what these verses mean and how it impacts the way you currently live.

❖ <u>Exodus 20:12</u>

- ❖ [Proverbs 30:17](#)

- ❖ [Colossians 3:20](#)

- ❖ [Ephesians 6:1](#)

- ❖ [Matthew 15:4](#)

As you can see, submitting to your parents is a big deal to God. So big, that it is the only commandment with a promise of long life attached. This promise emphasizes the importance of this commandment.

I decided to talk about this authority first because I believe that it is the most important place for us to start. Your parents (whether your biological mom and dad or the people who are raising you) are the best practice you can have when it comes to submitting to authority. I believe this for two reasons:

1. **You had no control over who God chose to be your parents.**
Unlike the other authorities God placed in your life, there is no way to make your parents not your parents. You can leave a school or quit your job to avoid some authorities, but even if you move out of your house, you can't change who your Mom and Dad are. But remember this: No matter what kind of relationship you have with them, God intentionally placed you in your family. Even if you are unhappy with who your parents are, God has not left you. He is with you, and His promises are still true in your life.

2. **They live with you, and they see you every day.**
Your parents have the power to govern how you live in more ways right now than any other authority on our list. Not only that, but you are under their influence a lot. Sometimes the hardest place for you to be Godly is at home. I remember a time when I was younger when my mom was talking to my brother and asked him why he was so good everywhere else except at home. His seven-year-old-response? "Well, Mom, I gotta let it all hang out somewhere!"

Maybe you have a similar attitude at home, but the reality is this: If you can't learn to submit at home, it is going to be impossible to submit to other authorities in your life.

Wondering how you are doing submitting to your parents? Here are some key questions to ask yourself today:

❖ **When you disagree with your parent's decision, how do you handle it?**
Do you kick and scream and slam your door when you go to your room? Do you text all your friends to tell them how big of a loser your mom or dad is? Or do you calmly ask for permission to express your opinion in a kind and respectful manner?

❖ **How do you speak of your parents to others?**
It isn't true submission if the first thing you do when you get to school is gripe about how your mom wouldn't let you hang out with your friends the night before. Speak highly of your parents to those around you. Remember: the command for Christians not to gossip *includes* not gossiping about their parents.

> Remember: the command for Christians not to gossip includes not gossiping about their parents.

❖ **Are you thankful for all the things that your parents do for you?**

It can be really easy to fall into the comparison trap and even wish that you had someone else's mom or dad instead of your own. When was the last time that you really stopped to think about all the things your parents do for you? Be thankful for the fact that you have a roof over your head. Your parents work hard to provide for you even if they don't give you money to go buy the newest electronic gadget. If your Dad irritates you, but deep down you know he loves you, be thankful for that. If your parents are both believers, be *so* thankful. Even if you are in a situation where you have parents who don't meet your needs the way you feel they should, remember to be thankful that you have a Heavenly Father who loves you with a powerful, never-changing love and who has not left you in the midst of this tough situation. God still has plans for your life that will blow you away if you let Him.

❖ **How do I represent Christ to my parents?**

Many of you doing this study do not have Christian parents at home. If you talk about Christ to your parents but do not respect or show love to them, it is going to be very hard for them to see the impact Christ has had on your life. Live in such a way at home that shows Christ's love to your parents. Even if you live in a Christian home, are your actions encouraging your parents to love God more?

Your parents are not perfect. In fact, none of the

authorities that we will be studying this week are perfect. There are going to be plenty of times when you don't think that they *deserve* your submission. This is when it is so important to remember that when you submit to your parents, you are really submitting to God which is an incredible, beautiful way to worship Him.

Take some time today to pray and ask God how you are doing when it comes to submitting to your parents. Ask God to reveal to you areas where you could be better.

Remember how I said there will be times when this study will be tough? Now is a time when I want to challenge you to take it a step further. Sit down with your parents and ask them how they think you are doing in this area. Say something like the following:

"I'm doing a Bible study on submission. I just finished the session on submitting to parents. In general, how do you think I'm doing at lovingly submitting to you?"

Take what they say and ask yourself how you can be better, then write down some notes below about some ways that you could show Christ to your parents through submission.

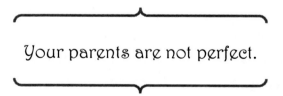

Your parents are not perfect.

Day Two: "Slaves, Obey Your Masters"

We ended yesterday with a challenge to submit to the people who are probably around you the most in your life...your parents. Now we will talk about the authorities that spend the second most amount of time with you: Your employers, teachers, and coaches.

Today, we are going to spend a lot of time looking at 1 Peter 2:13-25. Take a moment and read the entire passage so you can get an overall feel of what's going on.

You might be wondering why we are looking at a passage that speaks to servants or slaves (vs. 18). It is important to have a grasp on what this means in the context of when this passage was written. The Bible speaks of slavery multiple times in the New Testament. In the time period that this passage was written, slaves were treated as property of their master and were a big part of the economy. A person became a slave in order to pay back a debt, or because they were poor, they worked as a slave to earn a small salary, food, and a place to live.

Slavery was a reality of the culture, and so writers wrote to slaves and encouraged them to submit to their owners. The important thing to know, however, is that the writers of the New Testament required that slaves be treated fairly, and that masters not mistreat their slaves (Ephesians 6:9). In fact, every mention of slavery in the Bible was there to establish rules so slave owners didn't mistreat their slaves. Also, it is important to note that a slave was never considered "less of a person" in God's eyes, and their salvation was just as important as anyone else's (1 Corinthians 12:13). So, when you see the word "slavery," don't allow your mind to drift to the horrors of slavery in the U.S. in the 1700s, because people were not treated the way that the Bible commands.

Since slaves reported to their authorities, we are going to look at this passage in the context of the authorities that you report to pretty much on a daily basis: Your teachers, coaches, and employers.

Read vs. 1 Peter 2:18-20. In the space below, write in your own words the way that these verses say you should act when submitting to these authorities.

Wait...so this passage is telling us that if we have a teacher, coach, or employer who does not treat us fairly, that we should do good toward them anyway? Yes. I told you this was going to be a tough week. This can be hard one swallow, but look again at the argument that Peter makes starting in verse 20:

For what credit is it if, when you sin and are beaten for it, you endure? But if when you do good and suffer for it you endure, this is a gracious thing in the sight of God.

Peter challenges Christians to submit to authorities with respect *even* if they are not being treated fairly, because anyone can do wrong toward someone and endure the punishment. For someone to do good and endure the mistreatment of the authority is pleasing in the sight of God because you are remembering that it is ultimately God to whom you are submitting. Keep in mind that this doesn't mean that He is glad that you are being treated unfairly. The Bible says that God will take revenge on those who treat others wrongly (Romans 12:19). Instead, it means that when you submit, even when it doesn't feel good, it pleases God because you are choosing to obey Him even when it isn't easy.

> When you submit, even when it doesn't feel good, it pleases God because you are choosing to obey Him even when it isn't easy.

So, what does this look like in your everyday life? Take a moment and think about an authority figure who might treat you unfairly. How do you typically respond when they act this way?

Circle which of the following apply:
- ❖ Throw a fit
- ❖ Talk back
- ❖ Roll your eyes
- ❖ Gossip
- ❖ Debate or negotiate
- ❖ Cry (manipulation)

Let's practice a little bit. The following are three situations that often come up in my conversations with girls. Take a few minutes to read these and answer the questions below each one.

Sarah feels like there is nothing she can do to make her teacher happy. At the beginning of the year, Sarah had a huge crush on the boy sitting next to her so she had trouble keeping her mouth shut when the teacher was talking. Once she realized the problem, she apologized to her teacher and became a much better listener. Her teacher, however, still picks on Sarah. It feels like anytime anyone is talking that Sarah automatically gets blamed. Sarah also feels like she is graded much more harshly than other students, but when she talked to her teacher about it, her teacher denied it. After a couple of months of trying, Sarah decided that it wasn't worth it to listen anymore since she was just going to be punished anyway, so she went right back to talking and being disruptive in class.

What are some things that you think Sarah did correctly in this situation?

Read 1 Peter 2:18-25 again. According to this passage, what are some things Sarah did wrong in this situation?

Have you ever been in a situation like this? Write down some thoughts on how you coped.

Brianna is saving up to buy her own car, so she works after school at a local fast food restaurant. She realizes very quickly that her manager is close friends with most of the other employees. Over time, it becomes obvious to Brianna that the other employees are getting much easier shifts and responsibilities. Brianna has asked for Wednesday nights off to go to church, and the manager often tells her no in order to make the other employees happy. Brianna talks with her manager about it and nothing changes. Eventually, she decides she is missing too much church, so she puts in her two weeks' notice. The manager gets upset, and packs Brianna's last two weeks with awful shifts. Brianna decides she will just show up late, work just enough to get by, and then leave early since she is quitting anyway, and the manager doesn't deserve her hard work.

What are some things you think Brianna did right?

Read 1 Peter 2:18-25 again as well as Colossians 3:23. What are some things you think Brianna did wrong?

Have you had a situation like this? How did you handle it?

April loved basketball. Everyone agreed that she was the best and hardest working athlete on her team. Everyone, that is, except her coach. April's coach, for no known reason, just didn't really care for April. April continued to work hard, even though her coach wasn't allowing her to have much game time. One day, April decided that it wasn't worth it anymore, and she quit the team without telling her coach. She then spent the rest of the semester talking bad about the coach and even persuaded some of the other girls to quit the team as well. After a few months, the basketball team fell apart. They had a horrible record that season. April made it well known how happy she was that her former coach had failed and how much that coach really "deserved it."

What are some things you think April did right?

Read 1 Peter 2:18-25 again. What are some things you think April did wrong?

Have you had a situation like this? How did you handle it?

You probably noticed that each of these scenarios had a similar pattern:
1. Girl notices something is wrong.
2. Girl attempts to fix the problem either through a conversation or through working harder.
3. Girl realizes that nothing is changing so she retaliates.

This is a common pattern that I see very Godly people slip into. They realize that something is not right with the person in authority and often, through much prayer, they go and try to mend the situation. This is all extremely good. The sin occurs, however, after their attempts to fix the situation don't work, and the

> The sin occurs, however, after their attempts to fix the situation don't work, and the authority continues to be unfair. This is when they retaliate in other ways such as gossip, rebellion, or laziness, and they justify it, saying, "Well I tried."

authority continues to be unfair. This is when they retaliate in other ways such as gossip, rebellion, or laziness, and they justify it, saying, "Well I tried."

Girls, sin is still sin, even if you have tried to fix the situation in other ways. Just because you do the right thing and go to the person to try to reconcile doesn't mean that you have the right to gossip about them when it doesn't work. In Brianna's situation at the fast food restaurant, her sin wasn't that she gave her two weeks' notice, it was that she slacked off those two weeks in attempts to get back at her manager.

Look at 1 Peter 2:21-23 again.

For to this you have been called, because Christ also suffered for you, leaving you an example, so that you might follow in his steps. He committed no sin, neither was deceit found in his mouth. When He was reviled, He did not revile in return; when He suffered, He did not threaten, but continued entrusting Himself to Him who judges justly.

Pray today and ask God to help you entrust yourself to Him, the

Just Judge (James 4:12). Pray that He will give you wisdom on how to handle your coaches, employers, and teachers as you encounter them. Pray that you will be a light to these authorities, and that you will have opportunities to share the Gospel even through your tough struggles.

Day Three: "Let Every Person be Subject to the Governing Authorities"

It was Wednesday night, and I was busy getting the things I needed to prepare for our high school worship service. It was one of those evenings where I felt really behind, and I was so busy running around that I didn't notice our student pastor had walked up behind me. "Hey, I'm going to have to slip out and do something in the adult worship service for a little bit," he said. "Make sure you say something about the election."

I found it pretty odd that he made this request. Sure, the presidential election had been the day before, but what should I say to a bunch of high school kids about it? Did they even care?

Immediately after we opened the doors and students started flooding in I realized that our student pastor was absolutely right.

The person who won didn't make everyone happy, and the students were not afraid to voice that opinion loudly. I was amazed at the hatred and despair that came out of so many of them. Students who I have never heard gossip about anyone were talking about the new president in horrible ways.

Today we are going to talk about how as Christians we are called to submit to governing authorities, and yes, even the ones with which we aren't too happy. Open your Bible to Romans 13. Read vs. 1-7 and write down anything that stands out to you as you read the passage.

First, let's go over some basics to make sure we are on the same page. Here are some questions that might have popped into your mind while reading this passage:

Who are my governing authorities? Governing authorities not only include the government (i.e. in the U.S. it is Congress, Supreme Court, and President) but also the laws and those who are in place to enforce them (yes, this includes the police.)

But what if my government is corrupt? Did God want a corrupt ruler? Go back to last week's discussion on this and review. God allows people to be in authority, but that does not mean that He approves of everything they do. Remember, you can protest in a respectful and lawful manner and still submit to the governing authorities. If your government is *requiring* you to do something unbiblical or abusive, it is vital to do something about it (notice the word "*requiring*").

Sometimes our government might *allow* things that we don't agree with, and it is your right to speak out against those things, but those things don't mean you are exempt from submitting to your government as a whole. For example, it would be wrong for me to say, "I'm not going to obey my government's laws because they allow people to get abortions." But it is okay for you to respectfully speak out about issues you disagree

> Sometimes our government might allow things that we don't agree with, and it is your right to speak out against those things, but those things don't mean you are exempt from submitting to your government as a whole.

with while submitting to the laws as a whole.

I'm a teenager, why should I care about my government? Although it is important that we trust God even in the midst of government decisions that we aren't thrilled about, this does not mean that we should just put our heads down and be completely ignorant about what's going on in our country. If you aren't old enough to vote, you will be soon. It is important that you participate and are able to make a knowledgeable decision when the time comes. Our world needs Christians to make their voices heard, and who are willing to fight to put Godly people in governmental offices.

Let's look at the passage again. As we dissect it a little more, you will notice a pattern that we discussed in depth last week.

According to verse 1, who is our ultimate authority?

According to verse 2, if you resist governing authorities, you are really resisting _____ because He is the one who put those authorities in place.

In verse 4, the governing authorities are described as God's servants for your _____.

We see that God is our authority. When we rebel against governing authorities, we are really rebelling against God because He has set those authorities in place for our good. God is fully aware that there are people in government who abuse their power. You can see an example of this in all the stories of corrupt tax collectors who forced people to pay more money than they really owed so the tax collector could pocket the extra cash. Yet, at the end of this passage in Romans 13, what is an example Paul uses to describe one way Christians must submit to their government? Pay taxes. Like we talked about last week, God will hold those people accountable for the way they lead. Our job is to submit to them and trust that God will take care of the rest.

So what are some ways that you can submit to God by submitting to the governing authorities in your life? Here is a list based off of numerous conversations I've had with girls on this topic:

❖ **Stop complaining about the government and pray for them.**
The students I was around the night after the election were upset, and they allowed those feelings to take over. But the reality is that bashing the government, whether by talking to people face to face or blasting them on social media, is just plain old gossip. Posting your opinion about an issue is acceptable; just make sure you're not wording it in a way that cuts down the people who are in authority. Instead, pray for our government leaders that they would have wisdom and that God would use them to do mighty things for our country (check out 1 Timothy 2:1-3).

❖ **Obey the law.**
This might sound silly, but the reality is that Christians intentionally break laws all the time and tend to shake it off like it's no big deal. What does this mean for you? If you drive, don't speed. I know it sounds crazy, but the reality is that you can't get upset with a police officer for pulling you over when you, in fact, were breaking the law. Ready for another one? If you are under

twenty-one, don't drink alcohol. No exceptions. It doesn't matter if you believe that the Bible says moderation of alcohol is okay, or if your parents say it's okay. If you are under twenty-one, you are breaking the law by drinking, which means it is sin. Regardless of how silly you may think a law is, if you disobey it, you are sinning.

❖ Trust God even if things are frustrating and seem hopeless.

As Christians, it is important that we be involved and informed when it comes to our government. However, it is unhealthy and wrong for us to get so wrapped up in it that we become overwhelmed with fears of what the future holds for our country because of the people in charge. Remember, no authority can ruin God's plan for your life no matter how awful the leader is.

Ask God to illuminate areas in your life that need improvement when it comes to submitting to governing authorities. Pray specifically for the President and other government officials as they lead our country.

Day Four: "Obey your Leaders for They Keep Watch Over Your Souls"

When I was starting out in Girls' Ministry, I remember stepping into the office of the Director of Women's ministry with a question:

"As a women's director, if you could go back in time to when these women were teenagers, what would you teach them? What are the things you feel like you have conversations about all the time now, that you wish they had just learned when they were younger?"

It didn't even take one minute of thought for her to answer. "I would teach them what it really means to submit to church leadership and submit to their husbands."

The next couple of days are going to be a little tough for two reasons: (1) Although submission in general is completely counter-cultural to what our world tells us to do as women, these next two acts of submission are an entirely new level because they apply differently to women than they do to men, and (2) you will be tempted to "not worry about these things until you're older." Let me assure you that studying these topics is important even now as a teenager because you will be prepared. When these situations come up, you will have a foundation of biblical truths on which you can rely.

Today, we are going to look at submitting to leaders in your church. Before we dig into submission, it is a big deal that we lay a foundation for understanding the importance that Scripture places not only on attending church, but also being committed to a specific, local body of believers.

Take a look at 1 Corinthians 12:12-27. Write down your initial thoughts in the space below.

In this passage, Paul is writing to a church in Corinth pleading with them to understand the importance that each person plays as part of that church. He expresses the need for commitment and how the Christian life is not meant to be lived out alone, but alongside a specific body of believers.

In the Bible, the church is referred to in two different manners. One way refers to the universal church which includes every Christ-follower on the planet. The second refers to a very specific, local, committed body of believers. Guess which "church" is talked about the most in Scripture? The local one. In fact, entire letters were written to local churches, and numerous chapters are dedicated to church structure and how members of a church should treat each other. What does all of this mean? Being an active part of a local body of believers is a big deal to God. Unfortunately, there are a slew of churches popping up all over the place that have shied away from membership and even encourage church members to shop around. I believe this creates a lack of commitment that is devastating to spiritual growth.

Being an active part of a local body of believers is a big deal to God.

Even though being a committed member of a church is not the focus of this study, it's important to understand as we talk about submission. Why? Because if you never commit to a church, you will have difficulty submitting to the authorities in that body. When things don't go exactly how you want, you will be tempted to leave and find a church where submitting isn't as hard. This creates a consumer mentality of not asking, "What can I do for the church?" Instead we start asking, "What can the church do for me?" This is both dangerous and destructive in a believer's life. If you aren't committed to a local church, I urge you to look for one where you can commit and be active.[v]

The reality is this: The church is run by people, and people are not perfect. Your pastor is not perfect, nor should he pretend to be. The leaders in your church are going to make mistakes, they are going to mess up, they are going to lose their tempers, and make poor decisions sometimes. The other reality is that they are going to make good decisions that are maybe hard for you to agree with but they really are what's best for you as well as the entire church body. Either way, unless it's unbiblical, our call is to submit and help make it the best church possible.

Look at Hebrews 13:17-19. In this passage, the word "leaders" is referring to leaders in the church. Write down what it says in your own words below.

Verse 17 gives us a clear, no loopholes command that we need to submit to our church leaders. It also reminds us that they will be held accountable one day for how they lead.

Look again at the second part of the verse. Fill in the blanks below.

"Let them do this with _____ and not with _____ for that would be of no advantage to you."

When church members refuse to submit to the leaders in the church, it not only strips those leaders of the joy of their jobs, it puts the church at a standstill. A church that can't go anywhere because its people won't follow is "of no advantage to you."

So, what might this look like for you as a teenage girl? Here are some things to think about today.

❖ **Become active in your church as a whole.**

I see a lot of really good student ministries that fail because leaders neglect to remind students that the student ministry is not their church. Students should see that the church as a whole is their church. If you aren't already, become an active attendee of your church's corporate worship service. Maybe you're doing that, but you aren't getting involved in a small group of people who can get to know you and speak truth into your life on a personal level. Step out of your comfort zone and join a group. Serve in your church, both inside and outside of your student ministry or college ministry. Tithe, go to meetings, read your church's bylaws, get to know this place to which you are committing.

❖ **Always assume the best of the leaders in your church.**

Every year around camp time, I always had a least one mom call me, furious that I didn't put their son or daughter in the same small group as a specific friend. There were a few times that I would even have parents accuse me of planning maliciously. What they didn't realize were the prayers I prayed and time I spent creating those groups and placing their son or daughter in a spot that I thought would result in the most spiritual growth for them. But what would I spend a majority of time doing the week before camp? I would be stressed out on the phone with an angry parent, just wishing that he or she would trust me.

We need to trust the leaders in our church and always assume the best of them. If someone mistreats you, or if gossip is thrown your direction, don't assume the worst. Approach that person face-to-face and talk to them. Voice your opinion just like Jesus did in the Garden of Gethsemane, but in the end, trust his or her decisions. If it is a situation where sin is involved, follow Matthew 18 and grab another church leader to go with you. Don't just join in the gossip, be part of the solution.

> If someone mistreats you, or if gossip is thrown your direction, don't assume the worst.

❖ Don't run when things get tough.

Churches are going to go through rough times. You're probably going to have a church member say something hurtful to you, or you'll have a staff member accidentally neglect or upset you in some way. During my time in student ministry, I can't tell you how many students left our church saying, "I just didn't feel welcome." The easy thing to do is run away to the other church down the street that seems cooler or more welcoming at the time. The harder and more rewarding thing is to stick it out and be part of the solution. Don't feel welcome? Start looking for others who feel the same way, and be the one who welcomes them. If you feel like your student ministry has too many cliques, be inviting to people who are outside of your group. Feel like the church should host a particular event? Don't complain, offer to help make it happen. The point? Don't go to someone to complain, go with a solution.

❖ **If God really does call you away, leave well.**
There will be times in your life when God will call you to go to a new church. Remember, this should be a calling from God, not an angry reaction. If this happens, leave your current church well. Speak highly of the church and keep the commitments you have made. Don't use Facebook as a way to praise your new place in a way that slams the other. Remember, even though it is run by imperfect people, that body of believers is Christ's church. We should treat it with respect.

What I've listed above applies to all Christians, both male and female. There are, however, situations in Scripture where women are specifically called to submit to their church leaders in different ways than men. We'll touch on this next, but if you have further questions, I have added a list of great resources in the back of this book.[vi]

I believe Scripture clearly states that there are some roles in the church that God specifically designed for men. These roles are the highest leadership roles in the church, such as church elders and the teaching pastor (see 1 Timothy 3). This also means that there are situations that Scripture says it's appropriate for a woman to speak and lead others in the church, and situations that are inappropriate (Gal 3:28; 1 Cor 11:2-16; 1 Tim 2:11-15.)

Although I believe Scripture is pretty clear on this, there are churches that disagree. Let me first point out that this is not a make-or-break issue in Christianity. A church that believes women could have these roles is by no means heretical or made up of non-believers. They just believe a differently, and that is something for you to research and decide.

Before you get offended and upset that God would give you a different role than a man, I want you to consider the following:

❖ **Just because we aren't the overall leaders doesn't mean our job is not just as important.**
Don't let the title or control mislead you into thinking that men are more important in God's eyes than women. The Bible is incredibly clear that although we have a different role than men, it is equally important (Genesis 1:26-27, 2:18, Galatians 3:28).

❖ **If we embrace our role in the church, the church will flourish.**
It has been a pleasure for me to work with so many women over my years of ministry who joyfully submit to their church authority and do so in a way that encourages the men to be better and to keep going. What breaks my heart are the times that I have witnessed how destructive women can be when they try to tear down the men in the church in order to gain more of the spotlight. This tramples the men around us and their God-given ability to lead, thus crippling the church.

❖ **Don't miss the blessing in disguise.**
Our roles in the church automatically help us to remain humble and remind us that we are in church to serve Christ, not be the

center of attention. Our role of support to the guys around us helps squash pride in our lives and forces us to rely on God.

❖ **Remember, no authority can stop what God has planned for your life.**
Just because you're not the boss or someone makes a decision you don't agree with doesn't mean God can't do His work. Trust God, follow Him. He will bless your submission.

❖ **It is not all about you.**
Yes, I said it. The gender God gave you is not there to make you happy. He gave you your gender to bring Himself glory. We can find joy in our gender by trusting God with it even when things are hard.

> The gender God gave you is not there to make you happy. He gave you your gender to bring Himself glory. We can find joy in our gender by trusting God with it even when things are hard.

There is a lot to think about and pray through today. Pray and ask God to open your heart and mind to what you just learned and to teach you and humble you. If during this study you realize that you haven't submitted to a church leader the way you should, or you haven't gone and talked with a church member about a way that they hurt you, I challenge you to go and make that right to the best of your ability.

I feel the need to pause for a moment and remind you that unfortunately there are situations where men in church staff positions abuse the role that God has given them. If you ever feel uncomfortable with the way a staff member acts toward you or talks to you, run from that situation and tell a trusted adult.

Get prayed up! Tomorrow is another big day as we discuss submitting to our husbands.

Day Five: "Wives, Submit to Your Husbands"

A multi-Grammy winning country music artist started an Internet firestorm after an interview she had with People Magazine in their April 2013 issue. In the interview, she told the reporter that if her husband were to ask her to quit country music that she would do it. "When you make that promise to somebody, and you stand before God and your family and friends, you've got to do everything that you possibly can to make that work," she said.

That statement soon became the hot topic of the Internet as people chimed in with their comments toward this type of submission. Very few comments were positive, and some went as far to say that she was weak and anti-feministic to be willing to bend to the will of a man like that.

Today, we are going to talk about an authority that God places in your life that is the most controversial when it comes to the word submission. So controversial, in fact, that some churches have shied away from it, calling it a "cultural" or "old-fashioned" topic in the Bible. Some of you reading this might be so curious about this topic that you skipped straight to this chapter instead of reading the beginning of the book. I urge you to wait and go back and do the entire study because you need to grasp the topic of submission as a whole, not just what is written in this chapter.

I want to look at how this is a very real commandment from God, and why it is very important for you to understand even as a single woman.

First, let's take a look at some key passages that address submitting to your husband.

❖ Read Ephesians 5:22-33.

This is a letter written by Paul to the believers in the church of Ephesus. In verses 23-24, he compares the wife submitting to her husband to the _____ submitting to _____.

This verse is important for us to understand for two reasons:

1. It shows the importance of the wife.

Just because a woman is called to submit to a man does not mean that she is "weaker." Genesis 1 clearly points out that God created men and women as equal image bearers. Plus, notice how in this passage that the woman is compared to the Church. The Church is held with high regard all throughout Scripture as so important that Christ died for it.

2. It shows the great responsibility of the husband.

Unfortunately, we live in a world that has greatly abused the Bible's call to submission. There are men who use passages like this one as an excuse to be tyrants in their home, refusing to let their wives have a say in anything. Read verses 25-33 again.

In the space below, write in your own words the way the husband is to love his wife.

❖ Read 1 Corinthians 11:3-14.

These verses are commonly used to argue that wives submitting to husbands are out of date, just like the head coverings mentioned. A lot of women take great offense to this passage upon first reading it, but let's look at the facts.

> If God wanted everyone to have a man's role, He wouldn't have created women.

1. **This passage is not about head coverings.**

Well, it was when it was written, but you have to take a glimpse into church history to understand. Simply put, if a woman "uncovered her head" or "shaved her head" in the church of Corinth, essentially she was communicating that she wanted to erase the distinction between the sexes. Why is this a big deal? Because if God wanted everyone to have a man's role, He wouldn't have created women. Sadly, the people today who are telling our world that "women are no different from men" are basically saying that God just made us different so we can reproduce and that's all. But He created you as more than "a man who can reproduce." He gave you a distinct and vital role that He wants us to embrace, not run away from.

2. **It isn't just "cultural."**

What's funny about this passage is that although it is a passage many try to use to show women submitting to men as a "cultural" thing, it is actually one of the clearest passages that shows that it's not. Look at verses 8-9. Notice that the argument Paul uses goes back to creation, not culture. This is so important because he is pointing out that God created us for this reason. This form of submission is not something caused by culture or caused by sin. He created woman to submit and be a partner to man from the beginning.

3. We need each other.

Just like in many other passages, Paul immediately points out that it's not just women who need men, but men also need women. Notice how vs. 11 quickly points out that although women came from man originally, now men are born of women. He is reiterating the importance of both women and men working together. Then in verse 14, he points out that it is just as wrong for a man to try to take the role of a woman.

Our culture screams against this idea, saying that a woman should always look out for herself, always voice her opinion, and often dehumanize her man in the process. Reality shows are plagued with women who strip the authority away from their husbands and constantly disrespect them. But the reality is this... half of all marriages in the U.S. fail[vii]. What our culture is telling us just isn't working. My prayer is that we will stop believing the lie that we must be the one in charge and instead embrace being lovingly cared for by a man who we support in a way that makes him the best leader possible.

I believe a majority of today's struggling marriages fall into one of four different scenarios. Let's take a look at each of them.

- ❖ Daniel is a **tyrant husband.** He demands his authority in a way that is completely unbiblical. Instead of loving his wife, Caroline, like Christ loved the Church, he rules over her with an iron fist, refusing to allow her to have any say in what happens in the family. The result is that Caroline feels completely unloved, unimportant, and is unable to be the wife that God has designed her to be.

- ❖ Carrie is a **tyrant wife.** She rules the household and does not allow her husband, Sam, to make decisions. If he does, she either ignores him or humiliates him if the decision turns out not to have the greatest results. The outcome is that Sam can't lead, has no control, and can't be the husband that God has designed him to be.

- ❖ Anthony is a **tyrant husband**, and Courtney is a **tyrant wife.** This is a marriage in which they both try to lead the family and often adopt a "my way or the highway" mentality. This marriage not only leads to bitterness and a torn up family, but also results in Anthony and Courtney leading two, totally separate lives, refusing to allow the other one to have a say in how they live.

- ❖ Donnie is a **passive husband**, and Katrina is a **passive wife.** This is a marriage in which no one is taking the lead. Instead of making decisions and working toward the future, Donnie and Katrina pass through life never really being who God created them to be. Although they rarely get into an argument, both are extremely unhappy and wondering what it is that they are missing in life.

I don't know about you, but none of these scenarios sound very "happily ever after." If left this way, marriages in this state tend to lead to bitterness and often physical or emotional affairs. This not only destroys marriages, but destroys families, friends, and even churches. Couples like this aren't focused on the Gospel, they are focused on their problems, and our Enemy loves every minute of it.

Look again at Ephesians 5:22-33. Instead of focusing on what the woman can or can't do, I want you to look at the picture of the beautiful relationship that this passage is painting. This is the kind of marriage that God wants for us:

❖ Adam is a **leading husband**, and Janie is a **submissive wife**. This is a home where Adam loves and cherishes Janie and would do anything for her. He leads the family and makes the final decisions but takes into account Janie's thoughts and dreams. Janie respects Adam, always speaking highly of him to others and submitting to him in a trusting way that empowers him to lead better and love her better. This beautiful partnership is the perfect balance that allows them to focus on their love for one another and their love for Christ.

> Couples like this aren't focused on the Gospel, they are focused on their problems, and our Enemy loves every minute of it.

Does this sound too good to be true? It's not! This is the type of marriage God desires for each of us! What if instead of affair-filled reality shows, we saw stories of newlyweds who trust each other and treat one another right? What if instead of the divorce rate going up, we see marriages that have held strong for fifty years because the husband and wife choose to live this way? What if instead of couples falling apart during tragedy, we see a husband

and wife who encourage and uplift one another and stand together through the struggles? What if instead of broken homes, we see the next generation of kids being raised in homes where the husband and wife love each other like this? Girls, the Bible does not paint us a picture of "weak" women, but instead strong women who embrace this role and empower their husbands and families to be the best people possible.

But you might be wondering how this applies to you right now as a single woman. It applies in *so* many ways!

> Girls, the Bible does not paint us a picture of "weak" women, but instead strong women who embrace this role and empower their husbands and families to be the best people possible.

❖ It should make you think about who you date.

The Bible is very clear that Christians should not marry unbelievers (2 Corinthians 6:14), and the reality is that the person you marry is someone you date first! Be willing to wait for a Godly man who will lead you, and who desires to follow God. Don't allow feelings to cloud your judgment. Sometimes those feelings will be strong, but just because you feel something does not mean that you have to follow it.

Ask yourself is this a guy to whom I would be willing to submit? The person you marry is the man who ultimately will have the final say when it comes to big decisions. You want to submit to a husband who is submitting to God. He isn't going to be perfect, but is his overall goal to follow Christ? If you marry someone who is a tyrant like I mentioned above, you are still called to submit to him unless what he is asking you to do is sinful or abusive. You need to be asking deeper questions than whether or not he says he is a Christian.

The reality is this: If the guy you want to date is not submitting his own life to God, he does not have the ability to love you the way God desires you to be loved by a man.

Take a look at 1 Corinthians 13:4-8. This is a passage commonly read in wedding ceremonies, but the reality is that we cannot love someone this way. Only Christ working through us can allow us to love someone like this. Want to be loved like this? Date guys who love God and want to follow Him.

❖ Ask the hard questions before you get married.

When you find who you think is "Mr. Right," be sure and talk about big issues that will be important in the future. Questions about children, working expectations, money, etc. are so important to ask before you get married. Be honest when talking about these things and take time to pray about whether or not this person really is God's best for you.

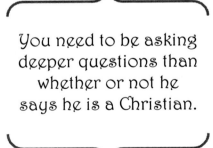

You need to be asking deeper questions than whether or not he says he is a Christian.

❖ Compare yourself to the Bible first, not your parents.

The reality is that if you have a marriage in which you submit to your husband, it might look different than your parents' marriage. For some of you, that will be a relief because maybe you have watched your parents' marriage fall apart. A lot of times we tend to emulate our mom's interaction with her husband. If you have parents who aren't following the biblical model of submission, be aware of that and constantly be in check with why you make the decisions you make. Ask yourself: Am I doing this because that's how my mom does it or because it's biblical?

❖ Practice submission now.

First, let me clarify: This does not mean to submit to your boyfriend. We are commanded in Scripture to submit to our parents and not submit to a man fully until we are married. Dating is a time for you to discover what you want and find the person that is right for you.

However, submission is not just going to automatically click when you become a wife. The best practice you have right now on how to submit is at home with your parents. Remember what we talked about on the first day of this week? If you get in the habit of submitting to your parents (whom you didn't choose), it will help so much when it comes time to submit to your husband (whom you do choose).

> This does not mean to submit to your boyfriend.

Next week, we are going to look into what it means to submit to one another. Take the weekend to pray through the things you have learned this week and to ask God for strength to apply these things to them.

Week Four: Sum it Up!

This week, we took a closer look at the authorities to whom God calls us to submit. They are as follows:

- ❖ Parents
  - ¤ Honoring your parents is one of the Ten Commandments.
  - ¤ Submitting to your parents is the best practice you have when it comes to submission because you have no control over who they are, and they live with you and see you every day.
- ❖ Employers, Teachers, and Coaches
  - ¤ Even if you are being treated unfairly, remember that God is who you are ultimately submitting to when you submit to these authorities.
  - ¤ Beware the pattern: Girl notices something is wrong. Girl attempts to fix the problem. Girl realizes nothing is changing so she gives up and retaliates.
- ❖ Government/Law Enforcement
  - ¤ Pray for the leaders of your government.
  - ¤ Obey the law and trust God with the leaders of your country.
- ❖ Church Leaders
  - ¤ It is important to commit to a local church.
  - ¤ Don't just complain about what's going on, be part of the solution.
- ❖ Husbands
  - ¤ Christ calls us as women to be supportive and submit to our husbands. This role is different than men, but equally as important.
  - ¤ This call to submit should change the way we look at the people we date now as single women.

NOTES

Submission Isn't For Sissies

Week Five
Submit to One Another

Day One: Submitting to One Another With Your Thoughts

These past few weeks, we have looked at what it means to be a woman who humbles herself in submission to God and the authorities that He has placed in her life. This week, we have one more topic before us: Submitting to one another.

Turn to Ephesians 5:15-21. Write out verse 21 in the space below.

This is actually a transitional passage that then leads us into the instructions of submission that we have seen in the rest of Ephesians 5. However, this week we are going to specifically look at what it would be like to live in submission to everyone around you. Yes…everyone. You come in contact with people every day who are not an authority in your life: Your friends, siblings, people at school, enemies, etc. Even though you don't necessarily have to do everything they say, God still calls you to a submissive lifestyle that will revolutionize the way that you interact with people.

Paul clearly defines this kind of lifestyle in Philippians 2:3-8. Read it and write it out below in your own words.

Look at vs. 3 again. What does it look like to count others more significant than yourself? Not just the authorities, but the people you come across every day?

This week, we are going to tackle different key aspects that we as women must master if we are to live a life that puts others first. We will talk about what it looks like to submit to others through how we speak, act, and even through how we disagree. Today, we must start this process by looking at our innermost thoughts. If we are truly going to submit to one another and put others above ourselves, we must first allow Christ to change how we think about one another.

Our thoughts are powerful. If we dwell on them, our actions quickly follow. This is why the Bible stresses setting your mind on the things of Christ, not the things of this earth. This is especially important when it comes to how you think about others. What you think about a person can (and most likely will) affect how you act toward them.

❖ Read Colossians 3:2-5, Romans 12:2, and Ephesians 4:23.

According to these three passages, what needs to be renewed?

So when you see a person, what kind of thoughts should you have toward them? Take some time and look up the following verses. Beside each reference, write down what the verse says in your own words.

❖ John 3:16

❖ Romans 5:8

❖ 2 Corinthians 5:21

❖ Psalm 139:1-18

These are pretty incredible passages. Isn't it amazing to know that God loves you so much that He sent His Son to die for you so that you can have a relationship with God? Doesn't it blow you away to think about how even when you were just a sinner that didn't deserve any grace at all, He still loved you and died for you? Let us never forget the beautiful words written in Psalm 139 about how God created us, loves us, and has a plan for our lives!

It is always a comfort to think about these verses. But you know those people with whom you struggle to have good thoughts? Those verses apply to them too. God loves them and died for them even though they didn't deserve it. Even if they haven't given their lives to Jesus, God still loves them, wants them, and might even use you to reach them. We must stop thinking about others based off of our feelings and think about others based off of the truth about who they are according to the Bible.

Take a few minutes and think about people that you come in contact with every day. Ask God to help you to realize how you think about those around you. I'm sure that some of you reading this are extremely skeptical about whether or not you can actually do this. Can I throw some encouragement your way?

> You know those people with whom you struggle to have good thoughts? Those verses apply to them too. God loves them and died for them even though they didn't deserve it.

Let's look at one more passage. Read Romans 8:1-11. In the space below, write down what it says about your mind.

Paul is writing this passage to the Romans to remind them that, as Christians, they are no longer a slave to sin. Their minds have been renewed and set on the things of the Holy Spirit. Paul says that, when you become a believer, your mind is changed from being set on "the flesh" (things of our sinful nature) to what is holy and Godly (things of the Spirit.) Okay this is important: This does *not* mean that if you ever think something sinful that you must not be a Christian. Even though sin no longer has power over us, we will still battle that sinful nature (Romans 7:14-25). What it *does* mean is that when we receive Christ as our Savior, the Holy Spirit dwells in us, and through Him we have the ability to understand the will of God and what is wrong and what is right (check out Romans 12:1-2). We still make the choice as to which to follow, but He provides guidance.

Why is this important for you to know when it comes to changing the way you think about people? It means that through Christ, you have power over your thoughts. No matter how difficult it may seem, with Christ's help you *can* control how you think about other people.

Today, pay special attention to what you think about people as you see them. Ask God to help you catch negative thoughts and replace them with good ones (Ephesians 4:22-23.) Train your mind to think highly of those around you (Philippians 2:3.) Don't get frustrated; all training takes time. Know that God is with you and that you can do it.

Tomorrow we are going to look at what it means to submit to one another through our speech. But as you will see, we must train our thoughts before our speech can truly be what God wants.

Day Two: Submitting to Others Through Your Speech

It was a typical Wednesday afternoon, and I was so excited to get to go eat lunch with some freshman girls at a local high school. I always loved getting to go to school lunches because I got the chance to meet a lot of new students as well as listen in on what everyone was talking about that day. The typical lunch chatter began: Too much homework, completely stressed out, what should I wear to the dance, etc. But when the conversation started focusing on the dance that was coming up, I noticed that one girl's name was frequently repeated. Every time this happened, a girl from our student ministry named Ashley would chime in:

"Liz? Oh yeah, I bet her hair will be perfect because she ALWAYS has to be SO perfect."

"I bet Liz spent crazy amounts of money on her dress. Her dad gives her whatever she wants."

"I think Liz bleached her teeth for the dance. It looks so fake, which is fitting for her."

I was bothered by these remarks, so when the bell rang for lunch to end, I pulled Ashley to the side and asked her what was going on between her and Liz. Ashley gave me a shocked look and said, "How did you know something was up? I promise I haven't told anyone what a jerk I think she is. I've been trying really hard not to gossip."

Yesterday we talked about how to submit to one another and how you must first choose to think good thoughts about them. Ashley thought that since she wasn't coming out and saying that she hated Liz that she wasn't gossiping about her. However, since her mind was still full of anger toward Liz, guess what was coming out of her mouth? Destructive anger and gossip.

It's important that we remember this as we dive into "submitting to one another with your speech" today. You can put the things into practice that we talk about, but if you don't deal with your thoughts about people in your life, then gossip is bound to slip out over time. Before we go any further, take some time to pray that God would continue to show you people with whom you need to think and speak kindly.

Now, let's look into some of the things the Bible says about how powerful our speech can be. Take a look at James 3:2-10. In the space below, write in your own words what this passage says:

Now do the same with the following verses:

❖ James 1:26

❖ Proverbs 18:21

❖ Matthew 12:33-37

The Bible is full of passages like those above that boldly speak out about the power of the tongue. Before we can dive in to how to submit to one another with our speech, the first thing that you need

You need to understand that the words you say are a big deal.

to understand is that the words you say are a *big deal*. I remember a time in my life when I thought I could say whatever I wanted without any consequence. After all, I was never a super popular person, so what did it matter? It's not like I was forming an army to attack a girl. What a sad day it was when I realized the destruction my words were capable of doing to someone's life. This is why the Bible uses such bold language when it talks about how we speak. We have to get it through our heads that our words are powerful. They can do powerfully good things or powerfully vile things in people's lives.

Today, let's focus on Ephesians 4. Read verses 29-32. In the space below, write down the words that Paul (the writer) uses to describe the qualities of our speech. Then, write down the things that he says we need to cast out of our lives.

Earlier in chapter four, Paul pleads with the people to be unified with one another, keeping in mind that we all have one thing in common: We are all sinners who have been saved by Christ. In this passage, he stresses the importance of not allowing our words and actions to split us apart.

Think about the things you have said this week. Would they all line up with what this passage commands us to do as Christians? Did your words edify (encourage, uplift, or benefit) people? Were they proper for the need of the moment so that they brought grace to those who heard them?

I love the harsh differences in the lists that Paul gives us in verses 31-32. He says to remove all of the following:

- **Bitterness:** the desire to cause pain. For example, "You're so stupid when you act like that."
- **Wrath:** Vengeance. For example, "You wronged me, so now you're going to pay."
- **Anger:** Feeling of displeasure typically brought from being wronged. For example, "You really tick me off when you act like that!"
- **Clamor:** Dissatisfaction. For example, "I deserve so much more than this."
- **Slander:** False words that tear someone down. For example, "Gena is such a ditz. I heard she failed her math test. What a loser."
- **Malice:** Desire to inflict harm. For example, "Did you know that Stephanie was caught making out with John on the football field yesterday?"

Instead we are to speak words of kindness that are tenderhearted and forgiving! I don't know about you, but I would much rather people speak kind words about me instead of the terrible ones above. So shouldn't we treat others that same way?

Let's say you analyze your words and realize they really haven't been great about the people around you, so you decide that you are going to change them. Where does submission enter the picture?

> When you are in that moment where you have something that you *could* say, but you aren't necessarily sure it is something you *should* say... submit to one another and don't say it.

I will make the argument that when we, as women, talk about other people, it is for one of the following reasons:

1. We don't have anything else to talk about.

2. That person has done something mean to us, so we feel like they deserve mean things to be said about them.

3. Our friends don't like that person, so we try to have the coolest, juiciest things to add to the conversation so our friends will like us better.

4. We want to make ourselves look better by bashing someone else. I would argue that this is the heart of why we gossip a majority of the time.

Here is where submission comes into play: When you are in that moment where you have something that you *could* say, but you aren't necessarily sure it is something you *should* say... submit to one another and don't say it. No matter how badly you want to look cool, no matter how quiet the car is and you just want to start up a conversation, no matter how awfully that person has treated you, submit to God by submitting to one another and choose to be quiet instead.

Read Proverbs 11:12 and write it in your own words in the space below.

Does submitting to one another by only using kind words toward others mean that you might not be as "cool" as some of your friends? Yes. Does it mean that you might have to be quiet more than you would like? Yes. Does it mean that you are a woman of God who chooses to love Him more than your popularity or your desire to get back at someone and that you will be blessed for it? Yes.

Spend some time praying over your words today. Ask God to help you to really think before you speak and to help you look for ways to lift up others. Be watching for people that you can love with your words. Choose to not gossip, choose to love.

Day Three: Submitting to One Another Through Your Actions

John was a freshman who, unfortunately, had all of the qualities of a kid that no one really liked. He was loud, rude, and unbelievably selfish. It seemed like everything out of his mouth was awkward, and a lot of times people didn't know what to say back to him.

It was so bad that every Wednesday night you could feel the tension in the room when we would announce where we were going to meet up to eat after our evening service. That particular night, as soon as we announced a local burger place, John was on a mission to find a ride. A "ride" not only committed the driver to a short ride to the restaurant, but also to the 30-minute trip to take John home afterward because his parents refused to transport him.

I watched as John walked around the room asking people. Time after time, he would be told no followed by the best possible excuse that a person could invent. This went on for so long that I was about to grab a friend of mine to ride with us so that I could just volunteer to take him, but then I heard Brendon yell from across the room, "I'll take you, John! Hop in with us!"

I pulled Brendon aside once we were at the restaurant to ask him why he volunteered. After all, as soon as he allowed John to ride in his car, all of Brendon's other friends found other rides. I'll never forget his answer that day, "Well, I saw someone with a need, so I did what I could to meet it."

Brendon showed me an amazing example of what it looks like to submit to one another through one's actions. Today, we are going to look at a passage of Scripture that shows just one of the many examples of Jesus doing the same.

Open your Bibles to John 13. In this passage, Jesus and his twelve disciples are about to have a feast. This is a big moment in Scripture because it is the last time that Jesus talks to all of the disciples together before He is arrested and taken to the cross. Take a few moments and read vs. 1-17. As you read, make a list of the events in the space below.

Jesus and his disciples were about to enjoy a meal together, but they were missing one important thing: A servant to wash their feet. In this time in history, most people walked around this desert region either barefoot or with really thin sandals. You can imagine how, after a long day of walking in the dirt, their feet would get pretty disgusting. It was custom that, when a meal was served in someone's home, they would provide a servant to wash everyone's feet upon arrival. This was not the most glorious task. In fact, it was often reserved for only the lowliest of servants.

I can only imagine the thoughts that were going through the disciples' heads when Jesus, the King of Kings and Lord of Lords, God in flesh, knelt before them to take the position of a servant to wash their feet. You can almost hear the shock in Peter's voice in vs. 6! But Jesus didn't want them to miss the important message that they (and we) needed to hear.

Read verses 12-17 again. Write in the space below what Jesus wanted His disciples to understand.

If I knew that I was about to die, there are a lot of things that I would want to tell my family and friends. If I only had time to choose one topic, you can bet that I would choose the one that I felt was the most important. What is the topic Jesus chooses to share? That they need to be a servant to everyone around them.

Let us not miss this extremely important message. We are to put others' needs before our own and serve one another. Why? Because Christ is our example and check out the promise He gives in vs. 17.

"If you know these things, blessed are you if you do them."

It's one thing to know that we should serve others, it's an entirely different thing to actually do it. It is a choice to submit to God by serving one another, regardless of how you feel about it at the time. God promises that we are blessed if we do.

What does this look like in your life today? Who do you need to serve? Could it be any of the following:

> It's one thing to know that we should serve others, it's an entirely different thing to actually do it. It is a choice to submit to God by serving one another,

❖ Allowing someone else to have the spotlight when you have worked hard to finish a project?

❖ Helping your parents with chores around the house without being asked and without looking for recognition?

❖ Walking away from your group of friends so you can welcome someone who is lonely?

❖ Being kind to a teacher who is not the kindest to you?

In the space below, write down some ways that you can serve others today.

But it doesn't stop there. Jesus takes the idea of serving others to a whole new level when you read verses 18-26.

Judas was in the room.

Judas. The man who would betray Jesus and hand Him over to the guards who would beat and kill Him. Judas. The man who followed Jesus and had seen all the amazing miracles Jesus performed. Judas. The man who had witnessed so much and was cared for by Christ in so many ways, yet gave Jesus over to His death for a little bit of money.

Jesus knew all of this was going to happen and yet…He washed Judas's feet.

So many times we, as girls, can get caught up in anger and grudges with those around us. We justify not serving each other because we feel that the other person has been so horrible to us that they do not deserve such love. Yet Jesus washed the dirty, disgusting feet of the man whom He knew was about to turn Him over to be killed. He gives us this incredible example, yet so often we struggle to serve someone because they said something bad about us or they stole our boyfriend.

Tomorrow, we are going to tackle how to submit to one another even in the midst of a disagreement. Let's finish by reading the following verses. Think about it today as you look for ways to serve those around you.

Open up to Philippians 2:3-13. Feel free to take any notes in the space below.

Day Four: Submitting to One Another in the Midst of a Conflict (Part One)

Grudges. Cat fights. Gossip. Arguments. Disputes. DRAMA. Like it or not, as women these terms tend to follow us. One day I asked a group of high school boys where they thought girls excelled. Sure, they shared some sweet answers. However, when I really got to the thick of it, one sophomore put it perfectly:

"They are really good at tearing each other apart. It's like with guys, if we get mad at each other, we usually blow up but then it's over. But girls fight differently. They are sneaky, malicious, and will never let each other forget the wrongs they have done."

The reality is not everyone is going to get along perfectly, and you are going to encounter people who hurt you and are just plain mean. So what do you do? How do you submit to one another in the midst of an argument?

Today, we are going to talk about why we need to understand that it is a big deal to God when we argue with one another.

1. **Fighting with one another is a big deal to God because it distracts our hearts when worshipping Him.**

I believe one of the most obvious passages that addresses how big of a deal arguments are to God is found in the book of Matthew.

Take a look at Matthew 5:23-24. Write what is happening in your own words in the space below:

Simply put, this passage says if you are doing something to worship God and you realize that you are at conflict with someone either because you did something wrong or they did, you need to go immediately and do what you can to solve the problem.

I remember a time in my life when I couldn't even focus on the words to a worship song because my mind was so full of hatred for someone. There was a girl from my church who had spread horrible gossip about me to a boy that I liked. I was so hurt when I found out it was her. But no matter how hurt I felt, I still had a responsibility to talk to her and get it settled.

2. Fighting with one another is a big deal to God because it destroys the Church.

Open your Bible to Philippians 4. This is an incredible letter that God wrote to the church of Philippi through the Apostle Paul. In this letter, Paul reminds the people of the church that Earth is not their home, and that they need to live in a way that looks forward to eternity in Heaven and draws others to want to know Christ.

Take a few minutes and read Philippians 4:1-4.

Did you catch it? A lot of times when people read this chapter, they focus on vs. 1 (stand firm in the Lord) and then skip to vs. 4 (rejoice in the Lord). But what is in between is so random that we cannot skip over its importance.

Read vs. 2-3 again. Write down what is happening in the space below:

It is very rare that Paul calls out specific people in his letters, but this time he describes Euodia and Syntyche, two *women* who are in dispute. In vs. 3, we see that these are not only women, but they are extremely Godly women who have greatly impacted others for Christ alongside Paul. What is Paul urging them to do? Stop fighting and live in harmony in the Lord (check out Philippians 2:2).

> Sometimes we tend to think that a fight only affects us and that other person. When we fight with other believers we have the potential to not only hurt one another, but also to destroy the unity in the body of Christ.

Here is what we need to understand: These two women fighting was such a big deal that Paul addressed it in Scripture. Sometimes we tend to think that a fight only affects us and that other person. When we fight with other believers (we will talk about fighting with non-believers in a moment), we have the potential to not only hurt one another, but also to destroy the unity in the body of Christ.

I have witnessed this in significant, devastating ways. A few years ago Gail, a freshman in our student ministry, stole the boyfriend of Paige, a sophomore. Paige, deeply hurt, quickly took on the attitude that it didn't matter if she hated Gail because they never really hung out anyway. She was wrong. Over the next couple months I noticed a rift forming between the sophomores and the freshmen. After a few more weeks, I didn't see Paige anymore and slowly over time, Paige's friends followed suit. To this day they are no longer involved in church. What happened? Gail and Paige, instead of going to one another and working it out, slowly allowed gossip into their lives. Eventually, their friends started to take sides. No, there was no "rumble" where the two grades started screaming or punching each other. Any outsider probably could have come in and not known that a fight was taking place. But over time, the gossip caused pain in their hearts, and Paige and her friends were the first to get fed up and walk away.

Unity is a big deal. It is such a big deal that when Jesus prayed for the church in John 17, He specifically prayed that we would have unity with one another (vs. 23). Jesus refers to the Church as His Bride all throughout Scripture (Revelation 19:7-9 is a great example). When you mess with the Church, you are messing with His Bride. As Christians, we need to do everything we can to defend the Bride of Christ. Don't allow separation to take place. Submit and go to one another to do what you can to fix the conflict.

3. Fighting with one another is a big deal to God because it distracts us from sharing His love with others.

Take a few minutes and think about the last time you got into a really big fight with someone. As you went through your day, what did you think about? Odds are, your mind was greatly distracted. It is so easy to wonder what that person is doing or saying, that is begins to fog up your mind and overwhelm you. What happens when this occurs? We stop thinking about sharing Christ with others because we are too wrapped up in our own insecurities. We start to get "tunnel vision," with our drama and problems, so we don't look around to see the needs of others. Why do you think in Scripture we never see Jesus going around and trying to fix the gossip that was taking place about him (unless it was blatant blasphemy against God)? Because He had a job to do, and He wasn't going to get distracted by what people were saying about Him. Let us not forget that we have a job to do, too!

When conflicts like this occur, we often drag others down with us. Don't allow your friends to get distracted because of a conflict you have with someone else. This is a big responsibility. Also, remember this: Drama with a non-Christian closes any door you may have to share Christ with them. It's not worth it.

Fighting is a big deal. Period.

We can't just ignore a fight and wait for it to go away. We need to become educated in the art of lovingly having a conflict with someone. Tomorrow, we will dive into the specifics of how to have a Godly confrontation. Today, pray about the relationships you have with others. Ask God to reveal any anger that you might be holding against someone. Start praying now about how to lovingly confront them.

Day Five: Submitting to One Another in the Midst of a Conflict (Part Two)

Yesterday, we talked about why it is a big deal when we fight with one another. Although we hope to never find ourselves in the position where we have to get in a disagreement with someone, the reality is that it is going to happen. So what should you do? How should you handle it when a girl hurts your feelings or even destroys your reputation? How do you approach someone who has hurt you so badly that it physically makes you ache? Luckily, we have a God that knows we will deal with these things. He provides us with incredible guidance. Let's take a look at a few of those things:

1. **Stop and pray.**

Take a look at Proverbs 15:18 and James 1:19 and write them in your own words in the space below.

When something happens that hurts or angers us, we must choose not to respond emotionally. The first thing we need to do is stop, pray, and ask God to reveal to us (1) if it is really something that is worth fighting over, and (2) what is real and what is emotion. There are going to be things that happen that hurt you, but after praying, you realize that it isn't worth an argument. Also, we are so good at assumptions…in a bad way. Sometimes someone hurts our feelings only because we read a little too much into what they said, or how it was said. We have to choose to be mature enough to stop and ask God to help us know if it is really something that is worth fighting about, or something from which we just need to move on.

> When something happens that hurts or angers us, we must choose not to respond emotionally.

2. **Remember what you deserve.**

Anytime I am angry with someone and I have a hard time desiring reconciliation, I read the parable of the unforgiving servant.

Turn to Matthew 18:21-35. Take a few minutes to get lost in the story. Write out anything that sticks out to you in the space below.

This man had a huge debt against the king, and instead of throwing him in jail, the king "forgave him his debt." In other words, he didn't just give the man more time to repay, he completely erased what the man owed. Does this sound familiar? Reread Ephesians 2:1-8. We deserved nothing but death because of our sin. Yet God, in His mercy, made a way that we could be forgiven. The heartbreaking part is that even though Christ forgave us when we were sinful and defiant, we so often do exactly what the man in this story did. The man who had just been shown so much mercy turned around and refused to forgive the much smaller debt owed him by one of his fellow slaves.

Girls, when we get into a conflict with one another, we need to remember to show one another grace because *we* have been given so much by Christ. So really, when you think of it that way, no one deserves for you to be mean and hold a grudge against them because you deserve the worst, yet Christ forgave you.

> No one deserves for you to be mean and hold a grudge against them because you deserve the worst, yet Christ forgave you.

3. Go to the person.

After much prayer, it's time to approach the person who has hurt you (or the person who feels hurt by you). How should you go about this? Again, Scripture gives us some great insight. Take a look at Matthew 18:15. This is a passage that is often used as a pattern to follow when someone is sinning and the church needs to step in and get involved. The goal? Reconciliation and repentance. This must be our goal as well. If your goal is to make the other person feel badly or to prove to the other person that you were right, this is not the right goal. Your goal *must* be to forgive and reach a point where you can be around each other again.

Matthew 18 reminds us of the importance of immediately going to one another, face to face if possible, and talking through the issues. This is not something that should be accomplished through a text message or other forms of social media. Ask the girl to go get coffee with you or look for a time when she is alone so that you can approach her. If this isn't possible, resort to a phone call. If that isn't even possible, write a very carefully worded letter. I have had to confront people in all of these ways for various reasons, but talking in person has always been the best.

Don't gossip about her, just go to her. Tell her what happened and why you are hurt. Be willing to apologize for things that you have done that are wrong. Ask the question: "Is there anything I can do to fix this between us? I care about you too much to let this fight continue." These are humbling things to say, but so important.

If the conversation goes well, praise God and move on (I'll discuss that more in the next point). But what if you do everything right and the person refuses to reconcile or they demand something of you that is not possible?

When I was in high school, I had a close friend who maliciously lied about someone very important to me. I confronted her, asking her to stop the lies. She refused and, in the process, completely and painfully blocked me out of her life. When I spoke to her again, she said the only way our friendship could be restored was if I agreed with her lie. I couldn't do that. I told her that I loved her, and that I cared about her, but that what she was doing was wrong, and I disagreed. If that meant our friendship was over then that broke my heart, but I told her that I was always there for her if she needed me or changed her mind.

And that's how it ended. I would love to say that a few months later she turned around and said she was sorry and things were good. That didn't happen, but I walked away knowing that I had done everything I could to reconcile the relationship, and that I had left the situation with the statement of "I'm here for you if you ever need me."

And sometimes that's all we can do. Whether reconciliation happens or if it is rejected, the next step is of utmost importance.

4. **Shut up about the situation.**
Sound harsh? It's meant to make a point.

Check out Proverbs 26:20 and write it in the space below.

After you have gone to someone and talked with them, *do not* turn around and talk to other people. The disagreement will never really end if you continue to gossip. This might mean that you also need to be willing to tell your friends to stop gossiping. You can do this by saying, "You know what? I've talked with her about it, and we are good. So let's not talk about her, okay?"

Remember when we talked about submitting to one another with our thoughts? When people come to you with gossip, you must ignore it and choose to believe what the person said when you talked to her. For example, if the girl with whom you were fighting has apologized and wants to be your friend, choose to believe her unless you actually see or hear *her* say otherwise. Then you can go talk with her again and see what's going on.

If the girl you confronted refuses to reconcile, then continuing to allow gossip will only make the fire bigger. Walk away from it all completely and keep your mouth shut unless you are saying something nice about her.

I experienced another situation in which someone wouldn't reconcile with me, and somehow it became publically known. I had many friends who came and would complain about her to me. It's amazing how quickly the drama went away when I refused to talk badly of her. The girl still wouldn't talk to me, but eventually everyone else stopped talking about it as well, and I was able to move on with my life.

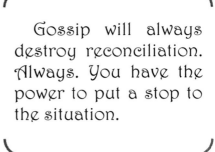

Gossip will always destroy reconciliation. Always. You have the power to put a stop to the situation.

Gossip will always destroy reconciliation. Always. You have the power to put a stop to the situation.

5. When necessary, get other Godly people involved.

If you continue reading in Matthew 18, you will see that there comes a point when it is good to get someone else involved in the conflict. This is an extremely rare occasion when harm is occurring that needs to stop. If this is the case, go to a Godly adult who can give you guidance. I always recommend someone older than you who is not directly involved in the situation so you will get an unbiased, biblical answer. Also, if it is a case where you are being bullied or caused pain, you should never try and face it alone.

When we shift our focus from drama and gossip to the ways of Christ, He can use us to do amazing things in people's lives. Just the act of you seeking reconciliation speaks volumes about the love of Christ. Our world expects us to be mean to those who treat us poorly. Let us be the unexpected generation who submits to God by humbling ourselves and forgiving one another so that together we can do incredible Kingdom work.

Pray for the girl (or guy) in your life with whom you may have a conflict. Take time to today to look for opportunities to talk with them, ask for forgiveness if necessary, work out your differences, and move on.

Week Five: Sum It Up!

- ❖ One of the ways that we submit to God is by submitting to one another (Ephesians 5:15-21).
- ❖ We submit to one another through our thoughts by thinking the best of those around us (Philippians 4:8).
- ❖ We submit to one another through our speech by only speaking highly about those around us (James 1:26, Proverbs 18:21, Matthew 12:33-37).
- ❖ We submit to one another through our actions by serving others and putting others' needs above our own (John 13:1-7).
- ❖ We submit to one another even in a conflict by seeking reconciliation (Matthew 18:15).

NOTES

Kelly Wehunt

Conclusion

This is just the beginning.

It is always a challenge when God teaches us things that force us to allow someone other than ourselves to be in charge. My prayer is that through this study, you have seen how submission is not only something that we as believers are called to do, but also that it is a joy because through it, God can use us in mighty ways.

God has a different plan for each of us. So different, that there is no way I could describe it here. My challenge is that you submit to God one day at a time. Those days will turn into weeks and years, and before you know it, you will be able to look back on your life amazed at how God worked. Don't get overwhelmed, just take it one day at a time.

Submit to God.
Submit to God by submitting to authorities in your life.
Submit to God by submitting to one another.
You will be amazed at His work in your life.

What is the Gospel?[VIII]

"Gospel" is a word that literally means "good news." And good news it is! Look closely at the words God, Man, Christ, and Respond:

God created us and therefore we are all accountable to Him (Genesis 1:1).

Man (all of us) disobeyed God and became sinful by nature. Because God is Holy, this sin separates us from being able to have a relationship with Him (Genesis 1:26-28, Psalm 51:5, Romans 3:23).

Christ came as fully God and fully man, lived a sinless life, died on the cross to bear God's wrath in the place of all who would believe in him, and rose from the grave in order to give his people eternal life (John 1:1, 1 Timothy 2:5, Hebrews 7:26, Romans 3:21-26, 2 Corinthians 5:21, 1 Corinthians 15:20-22).

God calls us to **Respond** to this truth by believing in Christ and repenting of our sins (Mark 1:15, Acts 20:21, Romans 10:9-10).

Do you want to give your life to Christ today? You can do that by praying and telling Him that you believe these things, and that you are making him the Lord (boss) of your life. After you have done this, talk to someone at your church or get plugged into a biblical church so you can learn how to grow in your relationship with God.

Discussion Questions

Week One Discussion Questions:
What Exactly Is Submission?

1. Before you started the study this week, what did you think about the word "submission"? Now that you have completed a week of the study, what do you think about the word?

2. The author defines submission as "the act of loving and trusting God so much that we willingly choose to follow Him and the authorities He places above us because we know that He is worth it." What did you think of this definition? What parts stand out to you?

3. According to Day Two, why should we submit to God? Which one of those points surprised you the most?

4. Take some time and walk through the three steps of submission that Jesus shows us in Matthew 26. What is something that you struggle with submitting to God? (Leader, help her to plug that thing into the steps and discuss them).

5. What do you think about prayer? When do you usually pray?

6. Do you feel like you can be honest with God about how you feel? Why or why not?

7. What does it mean to submit with joy?

8. Leader, share a time in your life when you needed to submit to God with something even though it was difficult.

Week Two Discussion Questions:
Submit to God

1. Why is it important that we learn how to submit to God before we talk about the authorities in our lives?
2. Did it surprise you that women are so anxious? Why or why not?
3. What anxieties do you need to submit to God? (Walk through the three steps on how to do that from Matthew 26.)
4. What does it mean to submit to God with your future? How can you do that in your everyday life?
5. In what circumstances do you find it difficult to submit to God?
6. What stood out to you in the "Submitting to God with my Appearance" study?
7. Which of the four topics discussed this week do you struggle with most? How can I pray for you?

Week Three Discussion Questions:

Submit to God by Submitting to the Authorities He has Placed in Your Life

1. How do you feel when you hear the word "authority"?
2. Of the authorities listed, which one surprised you the most?
3. Why should we submit to imperfect human authorities?
4. On Day Two it says "It's not your job to judge the authorities in your life. It is your job to submit to them." What do you think about that statement?
5. What is an example of something that you have been asked to do by an authority with which you didn't agree? How would you go about disagreeing with that person?
6. When should you not submit to an authority? Do you have questions about this?
7. How does submitting to the authorities in your life share the Gospel with others?

Week Four Discussion Questions:

All These Authorities... How Do I Submit to Them?

1. Of the authorities talked about this week, which ones do you struggle with the most? Why?
2. How do you submit to your parents? When is it easy and when is it hard?
3. How do you submit to your employers, teachers, and coaches? When is it easy and when is it hard?
4. How do you submit to your government? When is it easy and when is it hard?
5. How do you submit to your church leaders? When is it easy and when is it hard?
6. Do you feel that belonging to a local church is important? Why or why not?
7. What did you think about the study on wives submitting to their husbands? How can you apply these truths to your life today?

Week Five Discussion Questions:
Submit to One Another

1. What does it mean to submit to one another?
2. Have you ever seen an example of people not submitting to one another where it caused devastating consequences? What happened?
3. What are some examples of how to think about someone in light of Philippians 4:8?
4. What is the hardest part about not gossiping about someone? Why do we gossip?
5. How can you submit to one another through your actions? What shocked you the most about Jesus washing Judas's feet?
6. How can you submit to one another even in a conflict? Why is it important that we seek reconciliation with one another?
7. What has surprised you the most about this study?
8. What has God taught you these past few weeks during this study?
9. What are three things that I can pray for you as we finish this study while you try to continue to practice submission?

Notes

Submission Isn't For Sissies

Kelly Wehunt

ABOUT THE AUTHOR

Kelly Wehunt has been involved in full time student and children's ministry for many years. Kelly is passionate about seeing young women embrace who God created them to be in the midst of a culture that tries to steal their attention with lies. She and her husband, Chris, have two children who fill their lives with joy while constantly keeping them on their toes.

[i] Definition taken from *Called to Be a Keeper* by Lori Merrill.

[ii] All names used in this book have been changed to protect the privacy of students whom I love so much.

[iii] See the full article at http://www.adaa.org/about-adaa/press-room/facts-statistics.

[iv] Stats taken from *Graffiti: Learning to See the Art in Ourselves* by Erin Davis, pg. 20.

[v] I recommend *Stop Dating the Church: Fall in Love with the Family of God* by Joshua Harris if you would like more information on how to find and commit to a local church.

[vi] There are a lot of great resources out there, but I first recommend to look at "The Council on Biblical Manhood and Womanhood" website located at http://www.cbmw.org.

Several of the editors of that website also wrote a book called *Recovering Biblical Manhood and Womanhood* edited by John Piper and Wayne Grudem.

[vii] Some consider this to be a controversial statistic, however, even those that disagree state that the divorce rate is above 40 percent. The statistic referenced here is taken from the American Psychological Association. You can find the article online at http://www.apa.org/topics/divorce.

[viii] Some of this material has been adapted from *The Gospel and Personal Evangelism* by Mark Dever.

All Scripture references taken from the Holy Bible, English Standard Version.